The *Rosebud*
and the
Newlyn Clearances

Michael Sagar-Fenton

Truran

Published by Truran 2003

Truran is an imprint of Truran Books Ltd
Croft Prince, Mount Hawke, Truro, Cornwall TR4 8EE
www.truranbooks.co.uk

© Michael Sagar-Fenton 2003
ISBN 1 85022 183 9

Printed and bound in Cornwall by R. Booth Ltd
Antron Hill, Mabe, Penryn, Cornwall TR10 9HH

Acknowledgement
Thanks are due to the staff at Morrab Library, Penlee House Gallery and Museum, the Royal
Cornwall Museum, Gibsons of Scilly and the Cornwall Centre, Redruth for help with picture
research. Every effort has been made to establish copyright for the images, but this has not been
possible in some cases. Those ascribed to Morrab Library have been donated to them.

This book would not have been written without the enthusiasm and support of Mrs Patricia
Garnier, whose idea it was. She not only instigated it, but provided much useful material,
especially Geoffrey Garnier's three volumes of contemporary press cuttings. She has long
wanted the *Rosebud* incident to be given the full length treatment it deserves, and I hope
readers will share my gratitude to her for championing the project for so long, and for seeing it
through to a conclusion.

I wish to thank the staff at County Records Office, Truro; Penzance Reference Library; Morrab
Library; Penlee House and Penwith District Council for their help in my researches, especially
the latter who managed at the last minute to unearth some original archive material from their
legal files – though no doubt much treasure remains hidden there.

On a more personal note I would like to thank writer Douglas Williams, whose uncle sailed on
the *Rosebud*, for his unstinting help and photographs; Frank Ruhrmund, stalwart of *The
Cornishman*, for his childhood reminiscences of Street-an-Nowan; Hilda May Richards,
Crysede Tonkin, Liz Harman, Geoff Richards and many others for sharing their memories and
family stories with me; Jenny Dearlove for lending me her own research material; Alan Shears,
Tim 'Grevis' Williams and Betty Johns for photographs; my wife Liz and my good friend Simon
Turney for wrestling with the text and Heather and Ivan Corbett of Truran for supporting the
project from the start.

Finally I would like to thank the many others, who have approached me with stories and
details which I was not able to find room for in the text. I am sorry I could not include them
all. Their generosity is typical of the people of the port of Newlyn, to whom this book is
respectfully dedicated.

CONTENTS

A woman stands on Champions Slip, which with
its railings still exists behind the present
industrial buildings. The slipway up to Newlyn
Town is behind her, accessible at low tide over
the shingle. This early morning photograph was
taken just before the building of the South Pier in
1886 (Penlee House Gallery and Museum
Photographic Archive)

INTRODUCTION

I already knew the basic story. The little *Rosebud* sailed to London before World War II to save Newlyn from demolition. Like most local people I was rather vague about the details. Why was Newlyn under threat? Who from? How did the *Rosebud* save it?

Geoffrey Garnier's scrapbooks of contemporary press cuttings were a revelation. I had no idea to what extent the voyage of PZ 87 had captured the heart of the nation, filling tabloids with full-page photographs, prompting leaders in *The Times* and letters and articles from all over the country, a story which ran for months.

However it was when first studying the records of the families whose homes were condemned that my interest went from lukewarm to something near to obsessive. The records – included here as appendices – were like casualty lists from some major disaster, hiding a huge human tragedy. The discovery that some of the names on the lists were in fact only too keen to leave their homes only made the story more complex and poignant.

I would have liked to hunt down every last fact and to have written a full and exhaustive study of the impact these events had on a traditional fishing village. Time and resources did not allow for such an undertaking, and I must leave it to others to complete. What remains is simply a great story. The *Rosebud* incident cuts a clean slice through pre-war society, from the overcrowded tenements of Navy Inn Court, to the skippers and crews, their wives and children, the surreal world of the artists' colony, the prosperous burghers of Penzance, right up to the highest in the land. It is a section through a recent but almost entirely vanished world.

Within it is a narrative which contains dignity, pathos, irony and humour, plus something extra and uniquely Cornish. As *The Times* put it: 'These are Cornishmen, which explains everything, or (just as good) leaves everything inexplicable…'

Since it is being published within living memory of the actual events, I expect a wide response from those who know better, putting me straight about my many errors and misapprehensions. I look forward to this, and will try to make amends in time.

I am most grateful to those whose names appear in the acknowledgement and to the many others who have been so generous with their information, enthusiasm and support. My quest filled eighteen months of my life and made me ready to discuss the finer details of pre-war Newlyn with anyone at any hour of day or night, testing the patience of my family and friends. I would not have missed it.

There are no real villains in these pages. I am sure that all the characters saw themselves as acting from the highest possible motives at the time, even if the consequences were sometimes tragic. I have no intention of judging them from this distance. In the end it is a story full of the best rather than the worst of the human spirit. My own journey of discovery led me far and wide, but eventually back to the heart of Newlyn itself. It was a very special place in 1937. It still is.

1 'FIGHT THE GOOD FIGHT'

The dawn light revealed a familiar sight on Newlyn's South Pier. A small fishing vessel was tied up by the steps with its engine running, ready for sea. On the granite flagstones above a knot of family and friends were huddled. Often during the autumn season Newlyn boats would head for the East Coast herring ports and ply their trade there for weeks at a time. There was neither time nor money for trips home, and the women faced a long bleak period of loneliness and hardship, supported only by their friends and relations in similar circumstances.

But although this trip would follow the same initial course as those bound for Lowestoft or Yarmouth, its purpose was uniquely different. The little drifter had a crew of nine Newlyn men instead of the usual four or five, standing on the deck, made silent and awkward by the gravity of the moment. Fishermen, like all those who work hand-in-hand with danger, are highly superstitious and aboard the boat were a number of lucky tokens. A black cat roamed the decks. Safely wedged below was a bottle of water taken from the holy well at Madron. Beside it was an even more exotic prize, a bottle said to be filled with water from the sacred streams of the Jordan. A woman threw another lucky keepsake onto the deck, a pair of tiny red satin dancing shoes, which were picked up and stowed in the wheelhouse.

There were to be photographers present and so the children had been dressed up in their best coats and hats. More onlookers gathered, Battens, Williams's, Richards's, and other well-known local names. The Marquise de Verdières was there in person, and Geoffrey Garnier had motored down from Orchard Cottage in his open-topped tourer full of people.

A hymn was called for, and Billy 'Bosun's daughter struck up the old favourite of evangelical Christians everywhere, *Fight the Good Fight*, to the appropriate tune of *Duke Street*. Their unaccompanied voices were snatched away by the cold easterly wind as the light strengthened:

Run the straight race through God's good grace
Lift up thine eyes and seek His face
Life with its way before us lies
Christ is the path, and Christ the prize.

Prayers and blessings followed, and then it was time for the final goodbyes. The lines were cast off, and the tone of the fishing boat's engine rose as she slipped away from the quay. She left the harbour mouth and began to butt into the brisk head-wind. A wintry sun picked her out as she ploughed across the bay, seeming to make the morning even colder. The woman drew their shawls around them as they stopped waving, but remained on the quay until the boat was a shapeless object in the distance, visible only by the occasional spurt of spray at her bows. Gradually the little group melted away to their cottages, walking silently up the old slipway. It was not yet eight o'clock.

The *Rosebud*, registration number PZ 87, made for the Lizard, the first headland on her long journey east. Her hold carried no nets, but makeshift accommodation for the extra souls aboard. Her only cargo, apart from the good-luck tokens, was a leather folder containing a petition signed by eleven hundred Newlyn householders. The roads of the sea lead everywhere, and her destination was another stone pier, this time on the river Thames. The *Rosebud* was bound for the Houses of Parliament, and Westminster Pier.

With her she carried the hopes of families threatened with the destruction of their traditional family homes. She was going to deliver her petition personally, and 'fight the good fight' at the heart of government. Her chief opponents were not to be found on either side of the House or indeed anywhere in London, but in the arms of the bay she was leaving behind: in her nearest neighbouring town, Penzance.

The crowd on the end of South Pier wave as the *Rosebud* sets off on her mission
(Richards Brothers Collection, Morrab Library Archive)

2 NEIGHBOURS

The extreme north-west corner of Mounts Bay developed into a port somewhat later than its immediate neighbours in Penzance and Mousehole, probably because of the amount of soft muddy sand which accumulated there. However a quay was eventually built and a small fishing community grew around it, known in the thirteenth century as Nulyn or Lulyn, settling eventually as Newlyn. It was relatively insignificant – in 1337 the newly established Duchy of Cornwall recorded ten fishing boats in Mousehole for every one in Newlyn.

However its geographical advantages gradually began to tell. In the prevailing south-westerly winds there was always a safe anchorage in the stretch of water to the south of the quay known as 'Gwavas Lake'. The same can be seen today – the calm, barely ruffled surface between the port and Penlee Point, while huge breakers are hard at work half a mile along the coast. Penzance's harbour took to a wider industrial life and became a commercial seaport, while Newlyn stuck to what it was good at, and gradually claimed the largest fishing fleet in the bay.

Western Penzance and eastern Newlyn are only some two-thirds of a mile apart. Since the early twentieth century the sloping fields which divided them had been gradually covered with luxury houses, taking advantage of the sheltered position and the sea views. Now a stranger can drive from Penzance to Newlyn without any sensation of moving from one community to another. They are geographically the closest of neighbours, but historically – as so often with close neighbours – they have been the worst of friends.

Penzance originally came into being solely as a port, but at the same time a small market town grew up a few hundred yards up the hill. A thoroughfare, now Chapel Street, joined them. Both enterprises thrived, the fishing port branched out into shipping and industry, while the market town prospered and spread out in every direction until the two had merged into one. Seaports were not then regarded as in any way attractive, except when seen from a comfortable distance. Penzance was fortunate in being able to benefit from the success of its port without having to centre itself upon it. It was thus able to give itself certain airs, and gained a reputation as a town fit for gentlefolk, while the dirty work was carried on down the hill, out of sight.

Newlyn on the other hand was a fishing village of the plainest tradition. It moved to the rhythm not of day and night, but of the rise and fall of the tide. The harbour was its heart, and the settlement ranged itself around it, dedicated to the service of boats, their catches, and the men who sailed in them. It was an exclusively working class community, familiar with fluctuations of fortune, accustomed to danger and tragedy, protective of its own, with no airs whatsoever. Penzance people may have been glad to purchase its wares but they did not generally go there, or know its people socially. The two towns were as divided as if the sea flowed between them rather than before them.

John Wesley, on his first visit to Newlyn in 1747, noted how his open-air meeting was received with proper reverence by the local fishermen, but noted also the attempts to disrupt it by hooligans from Penzance. It was part of a long tradition of mutual rivalry, friction and suspicion. In 1795 a new harbour for Newlyn was proposed to supplement the original quay, but Penzance went to the lengths of sending a deputation to Parliament to oppose it. The plan was scrapped. In 1811 a similar proposal was put forward but again Penzance made every attempt to stifle the growth of its neighbour, and once again petitioned Parliament successfully. It was not until 1885, after the tragic loss of the fishing vessel *Jane* with all hands within sight of Penzance, that the need for a safe harbour of refuge was finally acknowledged and work began on the enclosure of the forty acres of the larger harbour we see today.

On the official opening in 1894 the Mayor of Penzance made a conciliatory speech, in which he acknowledged past differences and emphasised that he had come to extend 'the right hand of friendship'. However, two years later, an influx of East Coast fishermen in motor vessels who were willing (unlike their strictly Methodist Newlyn colleagues) to fish on Sundays, led to the notorious Newlyn Riots. It was no small affair. A naval gunboat and a battalion of the Royal Berkshires were sent to subdue the mutinous fishermen and protect the East-Coasters' trade. The Redcoats were surprised to find, marching at their sides, a fierce militia from Penzance. Some were enrolled as special constables, some not, but they shamelessly sided with the outsiders against their closest neighbours, and joined in pitched battles with the fishermen with the greatest enthusiasm. Old scores were settled and many new resentments were born. Shortly afterwards Penzance Council met in secret session and agreed to offer the East Coasters port facilities in Penzance, even to land the controversial Sunday catch. The right hand of friendship was firmly back in its pocket.

After the events told in this narrative and the trauma and loss of the Second World War, the two communities symbolically joined together by the amalgamation of their two formerly rival rugby teams into Penzance-Newlyn RFC, The Pirates. But it would take more than a token to heal all the old scars. Even as late as 1986, Penzance decided to set up a rival fish market, a venture which swiftly collapsed in a shower of debt and recriminations. Though the ambitions of the two ports may still clash, the old personal animosity between the two communities finally appears to be over for good. Newlyn Bridge is no longer a line which the young men of either side once crossed at the risk of a fight. Some Penzance people still regard Newlyn as rough and ready, some Newlyn people still regard Penzance as stuck-up, but the sting has gone, and they have learned how to get on. But they remain entirely distinct, and not always of the same mind.

3 'A PLACE CALLED NEWLYN'

Ancient divisions existed not only between Newlyn and Penzance but within the village itself. The village we see now is an amalgamation of three formerly individual settlements.

The most easterly, on the Penzance side of the stream, was Tolcarne, which spread out under the crag of Devil's Rock and spilled downstream. Its heart was the Tolcarne Mill, which enjoyed the restrictive practices of the time. Most local farmers were tenants of the family who owned it, and were obliged to mill their corn there and nowhere else. Though it can only be traced now by a few marks scored on a granite wall, the mill made a fortune in its day and was widely resented. However most of Tolcarne is comparatively modern, built at the turn of the twentieth century and plays no real part in this story.

Over the stream was Street-an-Nowan, a name which – unlike Tolcarne – has now virtually disappeared. It included the old slipways at Keel Alley and Champions Slip, once teeming with boats. They are now far inland, hidden behind industrial development, and the old foreshore is covered by the north pier and the fish market. It is hard to believe that the cottages which now look out onto a stretch of grass and a busy road once had boats tied up to their walls. In the heart of Street-an-Nowan is a warren of tiny streets known collectively as The Fradgan, stretching up towards higher Farmers Meadow.

The inmost point of the Newlyn right-angle consisted of a low cliff down to the water, and the largest component of the three, 'Newlyn Town', grew up in a semi-detached relationship to the rest, joined by a shingle bank at low tide and completely separate at high water. Newlyn Town stretched southwards towards Mousehole, clinging to the side of a steep hill. Below it the mediaeval pier created the first harbour, which survives within its successor. It was very much a village apart, with its own shops, schools and chapels, and maintained the largest population. Newlyn Towners lived in densely packed courts and squares near the harbour, as well as either side of the road to Mousehole, and in a succession of streets which climbed up the slopes to the west.

The three settlements shared a single calling and a single harbour, and lived in reasonable harmony. By the mid nineteen-thirties they had become used to the harbour road which first crossed the shingle in 1908 to join them together at all states of the tide. But even then they were by nature self-contained and kept themselves to themselves. Apart from the needs of business, Street-an-Nowan rarely went to Newlyn Town without a pressing reason, and neither went to Penzance unless absolutely necessary.

Following the opening up of Cornwall by the railway in the 1850s another community of houses had been built for more prosperous settlers who wished to enjoy the view without sharing the intense fishy smell, and these encircled the hillside above them all. In them lived wealthier middle class families as well as retired folk from up-country. Scattered amongst them were the most influential newcomers of all, the Artists.

In January 1884 the young Stanhope Forbes wrote to his mother from the Union Hotel in

Newlyn Old Harbour, c1884, unloading the catch straight on to the beach, where the carts are waiting
© Gibsons of Scilly (Penlee House Gallery and Museum Photographic Archive)

Penzance, declaring that he was touring 'in search of a more picturesque place than Manaccan' in which to make his base in Cornwall. He told her he was intending to try Porthleven, 'unless I prefer a place called Newlyn, within a mile of this town,' which he proposed to visit that morning. He did indeed prefer Newlyn. He fell in love with it at once and looked no further. The village was to become his whole life, and he was to be the most eminent amongst the array of talent which became known as the Newlyn School of Artists.

Forbes was by no means the first artist to settle there. Walter Langley was already well established, together with others, and by the end of 1884 *The Cornishman* reported no less than twenty-seven full-time artists in residence. Their discovery of Newlyn was an extraordinary twist in the history of a simple fishing village.

They came by a circuitous route. The centre of the artistic universe in the 1880s was Paris, and from there a revolutionary group had broken away to rediscover the countryside, and paint natural scenes and ordinary working people, working literally outside, *en plein air*. These artists, from many nations including England, headed for Brittany, where the picturesque hurly-burly of the fishing ports gave them the scope and realism they sought. It was not for some time that it occurred to the English artists that England had its own 'Brittany'. But they eventually took the long road – or train – west to see if it accorded with their visions. In Newlyn they found just what they were hoping for.

They all appear to have lodged originally with a fierce landlady, a Mrs Maddern at Belle Vue, who cherished them but would not let them touch a brush on the Sabbath. They soon found more sympathetic surroundings and studio space. Gradually the colony grew in numbers and influence. They found inspiration in the quality of the seaside light, in the boats and the business of fishing, in the higgledy-piggledy cobbled streets with their net lofts and cottages by the water's edge, their plain whitewashed interiors, and above all in the strong individual faces and forms of their occupants. By living amongst them they found their way under the skin of the village and painted not only a series of eyecatching pictures but also a faithful documentary of their lives, including the frequent hardship and sorrow of a fishing community.

Their appearance in the narrow streets must have seemed like the arrival of white explorers in an African village. Their clothes, manners, conversation and way of life were quite alien. They set up in public places with their often huge canvasses and set to work. (Newlyn's habitual shelter from the wind may have been one of its attractions, although the canvasses often had to be weighed down with lead fishing weights.) They chose their models from the curious crowds of onlookers. Despite their cultural differences, the artists and the natives took an immediate liking for each other. The Newlyn people could not understand why the commonplaces of their everyday lives held such fascination, but they respected the accuracy with which they were portrayed. The artists' models could hardly

believe their luck. In a life of such withering toil, the idea of receiving a sixpence for just 'sitting' was astonishing. They also appreciated the sympathy the artists felt for their lot, and such paintings as Frank Bramley's famous A Hopeless Dawn – often castigated as over-sentimental – struck a deep chord with those for whom such loss and grief were all too real.

The first era of the Newlyn School came to an end and many artists returned to the cities but enough remained to make a permanent focus of the arts in Newlyn, and a second generation of artists arrived, or as in the case of Harold Harvey, emerged from amongst the local population.

Although the artists were integrated into Newlyn life, it was on a somewhat parallel universe. The locals, while rather enjoying the fame they had brought to the village, remained slightly scandalised by their lifestyle, their Bohemian lack of formality with each other, their free thinking and (perhaps more supposed than real) free love, their 'wild' parties, and their lack of Christian – let alone Nonconformist – observance. Most of the artists lived on the fringes of the village or on the high hillside above, in some of its finest houses, Trewarveneth, Myrtle Cottage, Chywoone, Cliff House, Orchard Cottage, Pembroke Lodge, Penzer House, Maen Cottage and other beautiful locations where they built their own studios and houses. Dod and Ernest Procter were the exception, living in North Corner, a pretty enclave of cottages above the slipway in the corner of the harbour.

The Newlyn School artists' colony was an accepted and normal strand of the village. It did however set Newlyn apart, so that long before the era of mass tourism, Newlyn and

St Ives were well known far beyond the Tamar. Their daily round and the intimate details of their family lives, so faithfully recorded in paint, had entered the national consciousness The fate and well-being of these villages was – although it was not apparent until a genuine threat emerged – a matter of far more than local interest.

A friend of the photographer poses in front of the terrace known as Green Rocks which leads down to the South Pier in the early twentieth century. The houses on the right were demolished and are now a small car park. The house immediately behind his head was rebuilt and still exists (Branwell Album, Penlee House Gallery and Museum Photographic Archive)

4 'UNFIT FOR HUMAN HABITATION'

The first rumblings of trouble started as early as 1931, when a round of local government reforms was mooted, mainly to reduce the large number of traditional parish-based authorities. By the time this was ground down to Cornish reality in 1934, St Ives swallowed up Carbis Bay and Lelant, Camborne was unwillingly united for the first time with its old rival, Redruth, and Hayle ceased to exist altogether as an Urban District.

In 1934 Penzance's steady rise was crowned by the formation of a new enlarged Borough which put most of the neighbouring parishes – including the 'new' Newlyn parish based on the church of St Peter, consecrated in 1866 – under its jurisdiction. The balance of local power was changed forever, and the gravitational pull of Penzance superseded the old Parish Councils and Boards which had proudly administered their own populations since their foundation.

Almost at once the new Penzance Corporation began to address itself to the problem of sub-standard housing. This had been a central government priority since the end of the Great War, and was vigorously pursued by the Ministry of Health. The aims were lofty although the attitude was always patronising, and the language plain. The purpose was the destruction of 'slums', demolition of houses deemed 'unfit for human habitation' and the relocation of 'working class' people to new purpose-built municipal estates.

Nineteen-thirties working class people were mostly tenants rather than house owners. They were beholden to a small number of landlords and large-scale employers, most of them represented on the councils which made such decisions. Their own views on the quality or type of accommodation they occupied were almost never sought. Decisions were made in their names by various committees of their 'betters', and their part was to be duly grateful and to go where they were put. This was considered to be so good for them that nothing by way of dissent was envisaged. They were raw material for a succession of 'social engineering' schemes, which perhaps reached their nadir in the tower blocks of the 1960s. These schemes were always undertaken with the highest motives by modernisers and reformers who, however, rarely lived alongside those whose lifestyles they directed.

Penzance concentrated at first on its own back yard.

The practical sequence of slum clearance was first to identify the scale of the need, then find a piece of ground as near as possible to the town, obtain it – if necessary by Compulsory Purchase – lay out a new model estate, and then proceed to fill it by evicting the tenants and tearing down the appropriate parts of the town, which could then be redeveloped. The process was achieved with substantial assistance from central government funds.

Penzance first obtained an open area to the west of its public buildings, and laid out Penalverne Estate in 1933, before the borough amalgamation. Soon afterwards it began to look at its northern boundary, and in 1936 a Mr Daniel was granted a small sum in compensation for being prevented from planting his customary crop of cabbages in the area known as Treneere Fields. Greater things

A Cottage on St Peters Hill, Newlyn c 1890
Although this photograph was taken forty years earlier, it shows the typical doorstep life of the
Newlyners which was unchanged until they were moved up to the Gwavas estate
(Branwell Album, Penlee House Gallery and Museum Photographic Archive)

than cabbages were about to grow at Treneere, the largest housing estate yet planned.

Penzance was a prosperous town with plenty of employment and a relatively good standard of living. Nevertheless, like any town it had areas of run down overcrowded housing, and these were quickly identified. 'In Penzance,' declared the Borough Surveyor confidently in 1935, 'practically all houses are either reasonably good, or utterly bad.' A number of streets were soon condemned to fall. Among them were Jennings Street, much of which belonged to one (though not *the* one) Humphry Davy: Windsor Place, Garden Row, Cottage Row, Foster Place, part of St Clare Street, and later the whole of Camberwell Street, which ran parallel with Adelaide Street (now a council depot). There was negligible opposition, or at least none which reached the public arena.

So far so good. At the same time Penzance looked for areas outside its former boundaries requiring improvement. Its critical gaze naturally fell at once onto Newlyn.

The Board of Paul Parish, which previously covered most of Newlyn, had also been requested in 1931 to identify areas of unfit housing and to prepare a five year plan. Knowing that amalgamation with Penzance was in the wind, they managed to prevaricate successfully for four years, and then gratefully handed over the poisoned chalice to their larger successors. The first tentative visit by Penzance's Medical Officer of Health in 1935 was therefore the first critical assessment of the state of housing in Newlyn since a party of raiding Spaniards had visited it in 1595. They had found it wanting, being full of infidel protestants, and promptly put it to the torch. The Medical Officer of Health's reaction was a little less extreme, but the consequences of his visit were to be nearly as drastic.

To ensure objectivity the Housing Acts included a number of standard criteria by which a dwelling could be classified as 'unfit for human habitation' (the fore-runner of current Building Regulations). One related to windows, a formulated ratio of window size to floor area and height, to ensure adequate light and ventilation. One related to the basic structure, its adequacy and safety, fire risk etc. The most contentious – in this case – related to hygiene, which in practical terms meant the provision of running water and toilet facilities. The greatest curse of Cornish houses, omnipresent damp, was strangely not a factor.

There was also the matter of occupancy and overcrowding. The national standard provided the following definition of overcrowding of rooms per dwelling considered to be adequate for persons:

Rooms	Persons
1	2
2	3
3	5
4	$7^{1}/_{2}$
5	10

– and two further persons for each extra room. A 'person' was considered to be anyone over ten years old, while the under-tens rated a half, and babies under a year rated nothing at all.

The water issue was particularly divisive. Penzance had succeeded in providing running water and sewage to virtually all its homes, except those already zoned for demolition. The method of disposal was to discharge the sewage into the sea by cast-iron pipes just clear of its own foreshore, a means which was found less and less acceptable as time went by and tourism increased. However the

Entrance to St Peters Square in Newlyn Town. On the left some railings protect a fresh water 'shoot'. All the buildings in this photograph were demolished including the shop on the right. Standing in the same spot today – the first 'narrows' – you would have the only surviving houses on the harbour wall behind you, a public convenience where the shop stands, and the expanse of St Peters Hill car park in front
(Douglas Williams Collection)

infrastructure did at least exist. Much of Newlyn on the other hand still employed more traditional methods. These included drawing fresh water in pails from tap or a well or one of several free-flowing 'shoots', or streams, a tedious but customary part of the daily routine. Calls of nature were contained in suitable receptacles, usually an enamel bucket with a lid, and either emptied into the night-soil cart in the morning, or delivered nightly to the same destination, 'over cliff' into the harbour or the sea.

Generations of Newlyn families had found this system adequate enough for their needs. It may not have been pleasant, but Newlyn was a village steeped in tradition and saw little reason for change.

Penzance, in the everyday rivalry between the towns, had not failed to take note of the discrepancies in the bathroom area. It was part of local legend that Newlyn men could easily be identified by the red ring around their bottoms (from the bucket or Elsan), while Newlyn girls were known by the crueller elements of Penzance as 'ring-doves'. Penzance was able to look literally down its nose at its neighbour, whose natural waste products joined the detritus of fish bones, scales and fish oil in the water, sustaining generations of herring gulls above and crabs below.

It was usual for outsiders to Newlyn to regard all its occupants as an equal, somewhat primitive tribe. In fact there were just as many social divisions within the village as there were outside it.

At the bottom of the heap were the very poor, the disabled, widowed, orphaned, chronically sick, injured, insane, drunk or otherwise inadequate. Most of these were cared for within the community to save them from the cold charity of the Parish relief, but they lived lives of bare subsistence, some sleeping in rough shelters and corners, taking the dirtiest and most menial of jobs and living from hand to mouth.

Above them came the poorest working families, whose menfolk worked as occasional crewmen, farm labourers, or in the nearby Penlee Quarry, struggling to raise their large families on tiny wages, the men often away at sea for months on end. Many of these had turned their backs on Newlyn in the attempt to raise their standard of living, and took what work they could obtain in the industries, shops or offices of Penzance. The women took on whatever part-time work was going, as well as the labour-intensive grind of housekeeping.

Above these came the more established and competent fishermen with regular berths and marketable skills, some with shares in the boats they worked. Their work was long, arduous and dangerous, and their wages – like the prosperity of the port as a whole – depended entirely on the size and quality of the catch, and the vagaries of the weather.

At the top of the heap were the skippers and boat owners, together with owners of shore-based crafts and industries, in whose hands the fate of many of the lower orders was decided, a miniature aristocracy of established and respected families, many of whom owned their own houses.

To the outsider they all looked – and often smelled – alike. But within the harbour village everyone was well aware of their place, and their status was preserved as jealously as anywhere else.

Their dwellings also varied enormously.

Newlyn had grown in an organic fashion, bounded by the natural features of hillside and sea, taking advantage of what little space there was. It was a warren of human occupation.

Many of the old cottages and houses were handsome pieces of work, solidly built of granite, many founded on the old sea wall itself. Some actually had piped water, bathrooms and even flush toilets. With their bright morning sunlight and uninterrupted views over the harbour and bay, they were as pleasant as any houses in Cornwall.

The smaller cottages were more closely packed together, low and dark, and often very cramped with large families. However the pride and hard labour of the housewives, usually kept the walls white, the floors sanded and clean, the stove blacked and tidy, the clothes mended, the children fed and as clean as possible, and self-respect maintained.

Other areas were even more densely packed with 'courts' and squares. This arrangement can still be seen in Mousehole, where the first few doors in any street may lead into individual cottages while the next identical doorway may instead open into an enclosure with half a dozen dwellings ranged around it, hidden from outside view. Often these were built over cobbled fish 'cellars'.

Fish cellars were in fact on ground level, and dated from the golden era of the pilchard fishery. Then millions of fish would pass through the village every year and, in a period without refrigeration, had to be processed without delay. They were cleaned, salted, arranged in casks and pressed until the oil poured out for collection. The casks were filled up and taken away to be shipped abroad. Each cellar was a miniature factory. The family accommodation was directly above, mostly constructed of wood, often balanced on a few tall granite pillars, in a permanent atmosphere of fish, fish oil, blood, and brine, cold in winter and plagued by smells and flies in summer.

The courts were crowded to their limits. Families of six or eight lived in two rooms, a day room and a bedroom. Any building with a roof, a door and a window could become a dwelling, since they needed no services. Electricity was still rare in Newlyn, water and sewage were not laid on and there was no gas. Some had built-in fireplaces, while others made do with stoves of coal or paraffin. Those without ovens of their own used communal bakehouses to cook their pies and pasties, bread and buns. Such windows as existed looked out directly at their neighbours' walls. The hillside which protects Newlyn from the storms also ensures an early sunset all year round, and the court dwellings were always dark and gloomy. Tall (and not always vertical) brick chimneys sprouted from the roofs, burning cheap coal and creating a constant haze of smoke. Cleanliness in such surroundings was a constant battle. There was also no privacy at all, when the walls between one neighbour and another might be made of no more than planking or boxwood. The streets were full of washing as well as cats, dogs, gulls, and children for whom they were the only playground. Gardens were an unknown luxury – there was hardly an open patch of grass in the whole village.

Nonetheless, even in the courts and squares, mutual support sustained most of the population at a standard of living which defied the surroundings. Serious disease had visited Newlyn only once, the disastrous outbreak of cholera in 1832, part of a national epidemic. A sailor had carried the disease back from Ireland and before the end of the year over eighty people had been laid in a specially designated burial field at Paul. The only lasting legacy had been in the name of one of the courts which changed its name – at first humorously and then officially – from Coronation to Vaccination Court.

Unlike the slums of the big cities, the air was at least breathable and the outdoor life of the children was generally healthy. Everybody knew everybody else. There were chains of relatives of several generations, so that much of the village was inter-related and the very old and very young always had someone willing to look after them. It was no paradise but the very closeness meant that no-one's cry went unheard, no-one starved, and there was little crime. The 'master' of all was not a distant factory-owner but a greater power, the sea. The whole village lived in its service and vulnerable to its bounty or cruelty, and this united the greatest with the least. Strict Christian rigour set the tone, although hard liquor often eased the ways (in the heyday of the fish cellars woman and girls were paid threepence an hour and allowed a glass of brandy every six hours, brandy being relatively cheap and plentiful in a seaport with so many continental connections).

A few areas of the village could be described as slums by anyone's definition. There the darkness, the pervasive damp, the stuffy air, the rickety state of the buildings, the rats and mice, the noise and the smell were too much for the occupants. They lived in the conditions anticipated by their 'betters', dirty, hungry, ill-fed and clothed, desperate, in dismal resentment of their lot in life and of their landlords.

But mostly the poverty was endured as a common lot, with forbearance and good humour. The women met at the shops, the communal bakehouses, the 'shoots' where the worst of the fishy dirt was washed out of the clothes, the communal mangles, the water pumps and the schools. The men were inclined for rest when ashore, but attended improving lectures and talks as well as the pubs (the most devout via the back door). Nearly all met regularly in Chapel, two or three times on Sunday and at less formal Saturday night meetings.

In general the community lived ordinary lives and had a pride in the achievement of maintaining their own standards and raising their families.

To an outsider, with the standards of a more modern and prosperous world, it might all appear rather primitive, or even squalid.

5 BATTLE JOINED

How the Medical Officer of Health and his assistant were received in Newlyn is not known, but presumably it was with the same mixture of deference and suspicion which greets all official visitors. They went from house to house, climbed steps, stairs and ladders, avoided drains, made notes and kept their counsel. The MOH's first report to the Housing Committee of the Borough Council was however quite unequivocal.

The Committee's remit was:

1) To list areas in which clearance is necessary, number of houses and inhabitants.
2) List areas in which improvement by way of reconditioning is necessary
3) Make a timetable for carrying out repairs or rehousing the occupants
4) Make a declaration of such areas, and issue the necessary orders.

The MOH, Richard Lawry, reported that he had already visited about one hundred houses in Newlyn, and baldly stated that in his opinion nearly all of them were totally unfit for human habitation. His tone implied that he had little expectation of improvement in the houses yet unseen. Clearly a major need had been identified.

Scenting controversy, he asked to be accompanied on the rest of his tour by a suitable sub-committee. An alderman and two councillors were deputed to join him and made their dignified progress through the narrow lanes and passages of the village. Housewife after housewife was visited, her humble dwelling inspected to its darkest corners, and close questions asked about her cleanliness, toilet arrangements, the incidence of lice and vermin in her home, and other domestic intimacies.

Throughout the early part of 1936 Newlyn braced itself for the inspectors' verdict. Events high above the village showed clearly enough which way the wind was blowing.

In accordance with their instructions, the County Surveyor's office had been poring over the map of Newlyn and its outskirts. The problem was relatively simple, since they had almost unlimited powers to purchase whatever they wished. They disregarded the option of extending the village in the Tolcarne area by driving an estate up Newlyn Coombe (this was done in the 1960s by private developers). There was an obvious open triangle beside the hill to Paul, but it was occupied by too many private dwellings. Instead they settled on the next convenient area of adjacent ground, a wedge-shaped group of eight fields bounded by Paul (Chywoone) Hill and Gwavas Lane, between the farms of Gwavas and Trewarveneth. It amounted to some twenty acres, sufficient for almost two hundred and fifty houses: an ideal plan. Or so it seemed in the County Surveyor's office in Bodmin.

The problem lay, however, not in the plan but in the elevation. The hill above Newlyn Town is impressively long and steep, more than one-in-five in places, and climbs up some three hundred and fifty feet in half a mile. However short the walk from the old village to the new estate, the extreme slope turns it into a considerable journey, not lightly undertaken. The rigour of the journey discourages the idea of popping back and forth to the village without a good reason, and effectively cuts off the higher ground from the lower. For the elderly or sick, or those encumbered by small children and baskets of shopping (there were to be no shops on the new estate) it was an almost insuperable barrier.

There were many other differences. The higher ground has far more natural light and a great deal more fresh air – often too fresh in fact, as it is subject to frequent winter gales, rare under the shelter of the hill. It is on the edge of pleasant open country. The proposed density of the estate was about twelve houses to the acre, as opposed to the village, where it was forty or more. The houses would all have large gardens, as opposed to none at all below. They would of course all boast running water and indoor bathrooms. The estate was to be laid out imaginatively, not in lines and squares but with wide sweeping roads and crescents. Many of the houses would have a pleasant view over Mounts Bay.

Negotiations were commenced to purchase the land from Trewarveneth Farm, which was then owned by the Le Grice family of Trereife. The family were not immediately willing, and a public hearing was held to air any objections. The family's grievance turned out to be a reluctance to put a finite boundary to the burgeoning Penlee Quarry nearby, in which they also held a controlling interest. A deal was struck and the site was bought (for £3,676, which included compensation or the loss of quarrying ground) and tenders were immediately invited for the construction. The estate was to be named after the area in which it lay, a Cornish word meaning winter quarters or housing for cattle, gwavas.

Over a period of months, while the official delegation made its thorough way through the alleyways of the village, high above them the green hillside began to break up. The Cornish stone hedges were taken away in cartloads to other farms. The grass was either lifted or ploughed in, the topsoil removed, and a brown expanse was suddenly defined, filled with labouring men, lorries, and a few machines. The pattern of streets appeared, firstly only in string lines. Trenches were dug, with varying levels of difficulty – the rock quarried in Penlee was hard, adamant to almost every human device except dynamite. The villagers wandered up the hill in the evenings after work to inspect the progress of the works, with mixed feelings. As the estate grew, the deliberations of the Housing Committee neared a conclusion.

Their first pronouncement had in fact already appeared in 1935, and to no-one's surprise it centred on the group of buildings known as Navy Inn Court. The Navy Inn had once been a popular pub, just above the slipway which later became the South Pier. Like the Keigwin Arms which still stands as a private house in Mousehole, it had a porch set out on pillars with a room above. This was known as the 'balcony', which was pronounced for unknown reasons as the bal-cony, with the emphasis on the second syllable. The inn had long ago ceased trading and had been converted to a warren of flats and rooms, in which six occupied flats were home for twenty-nine people. It was already a local disgrace.

Like many of the rented properties it was owned by a prominent Penzance family. Penzance might not have considered Newlyn as its equal, but it was not averse to profiting from its inhabitants. The properties were bought for a song and probably never visited by their owners, but they brought in three or four shillings a week for each dwelling, a useful and reliable source of income.

The Navy Inn Court Order of 1935 included

The Bal-cony, the old Navy Inn, in what is now Higher Green Street. The whole of the terrace on the left was destroyed (see p74) but the house at the rear, Tonkin's Cottage, still stands (Morrab Library Archive)

some of the neighbouring properties which were also considered sub-standard. They included some houses in Green Street, a few at the bottom of Bowjey Hill (as it was then spelt), Factory Square and the long run of timber-clad fish cellars called Factory Row, previously (and less correctly) known as Sambo's Row.

Factory Row was the former site of the Crysède factory, which had been one of the few industries in Newlyn completely unrelated to fishing. It had been started by the artist Alec Walker, and was based on the hand printing of silks with new and revolutionary designs. Like Laura Ashley in the 1960s it started as a cottage industry but caught the public imagination and ended up with a large network of shops around England. Its success was its downfall as far as Newlyn was concerned. In 1926 Walker joined in partnership with Tom Heron (father of Patrick Heron) and they agreed that the Newlyn premises could no longer accommodate their burgeoning business. They moved to a large fish factory on the Island at St Ives, taking only their key staff, and many Newlyn women lost a vital source of income. After the departure of the factory the buildings were snapped up by a local landowner, barely refurbished, and re-tenanted.

The Navy Inn Court Order went through without a hitch, the only one to do so. The properties were condemned and their occupants were removed to Gwavas as soon as there were houses there to accommodate them, its first residents. Everyone was out by the end of 1937, and the buildings were torn down in the spring of 1939, when the layout of the existing buildings was approved. It was fully realised as a redevelopment, comprising rectangular blocks of flats with clear space around them. The buildings which now stand as Navy Inn Court and Bowjey Court give a precise flavour of the style of property with which much – most – of old Newlyn was intended to be replaced.

Had the authorities paused there, having dealt with the obvious sore spots, there would have been no trouble. Other ill-kept dwellings could have been picked out a few at a time, sanitation could have been slowly introduced, and the best of the village appreciated for what it was and preserved. But they had bigger ideas.

The idea that Penzance Borough Council had, together with the County authorities, conceived a larger agenda for Newlyn was never officially admitted. At every point the Council were to insist that they were dealing with individual houses and courts on a case-by-case basis, on a strict criterion of pre-set standards of hygiene. However their thinking would have been influenced by the prevailing ethos of the time, in which modernisation was all the rage. The past was not normally considered worthy of conservation unless it was in the form of classically admirable architecture. Vernacular charm was an esoteric concept, certainly in municipal planning offices. 'Conservation' and 'environment' were still obscure words in the dictionary. The main focus of this zeal was of course the inner city slum, and all over the country new estates were springing up and old quarters of towns were disappearing. The garden suburb was the paradigm, and models of town planning tended towards futuristic batches of well-spaced large scale dwellings surrounded by broad verges and parks, with a strong emphasis on roads and even airports.

Newlyn was not at all comparable with the classic industrial city slums. There were conditions regarded as primitive, but these were often capable of improvement, if improvement had been the objective. But it is clear enough that an overall strategy for Newlyn was secretly decided at an early stage.

The writer James Boswell on visiting St Michaels Mount in 1792 wrote that it was 'a disgusting shame to have a parcel of low dirty fisher-folk collected there' in the village on the island, and urged the St Aubyn family to 'remove the town'. It was another eighty years before his suggestion was followed, but the whole village was eventually destroyed, the fishermen sent away, and the model village which now exists on the Mount took its place. The conclusion reached by the great and good regarding Newlyn was effectively the same as Boswell's, that the only way to achieve substantial improvements in such a cramped and crowded site was to draw a line within a certain radius of the harbour and, with a few worthy exceptions, to demolish every single dwelling within it; to 'remove the town' altogether, and lay it out afresh. In one of the few statements to escape the planners at an early stage, the parts of central Newlyn recommended for demolition were not described in terms of houses or even streets, but in acres. To achieve the desired result, they thought, it would be necessary to clear approximately 6 3/4 acres of the old village.

Roads were a high priority. Few locals possessed cars, and apart from buses, vans, lorries and occasional tourers, the streets were still quiet. However the car was an integral part of modernisation, and developers were advised to seize the chance to widen and straighten their roads when the opportunity presented itself. Street-an-Nowan had already received its by-pass in the form of the harbour road in 1908, but the road through Newlyn Town was still serpentine and narrow. The amount of usable space between the steep

hillside and the cliff was very limited, with little scope for a major highway. The highway only led, in fact, to the even smaller village of Mousehole, and the average traffic count consisted of (as was later pointed out) 'one Western National bus per hour'. But if the village was to be largely demolished, a more logical road system was central to its replacement. Therefore a number of houses which could not be faulted on their own merits were regarded with equal disfavour simply because they obstructed the line.

Whatever the unpublished agenda, the first real shots in the battle for Newlyn were fired on 23rd September 1936. The following Compulsory Purchase Orders were issued:

Lower Green St Order No 1
Lower Green St Order No 2
Lower Green St Order No 3
Fore St Order No1
Fore St Order No2
Vaccination Court
St Peters Hill Order No 1
St Peters Hill Order No 2

The wording of the orders was invariable:

Having considered official representations under the Housing Act of 1936 it is resolved that:
1)   The dwelling houses in these areas are by reason of disrepair or sanitary defects unfit for human habitation, or are by reason of their bad arrangement or the narrowness or bad arrangement of the streets dangerous or injurious to the health of the inhabitants of the areas and that the other buildings in the areas are for like reasons dangerous or injurious to the health of the said inhabitants
2)   That the most satisfactory method of dealing with the conditions in the areas is the demolition of all the buildings in the areas.

The axe had begun to swing.

From the beginning the condemned areas were divided into two categories. Those considered to be obvious 'slum' areas were designated on the accompanying maps shaded in pink. These were the houses, cottages, terraces and courts which had failed the standard criteria, mostly tenanted but a few owner-occupied, and were thought to be irreparable.

However the pattern provided by the pink stains was not encouraging to those looking for sweeping changes. There might be one dwelling within a court which satisfied the criteria, or a satisfactory cottage in the middle of a condemned row. Or one condemned house might appear in the middle of a cluster of worthier properties, inaccessible from all sides. Many of the dwellings were structurally dependent on each other, and could not be so easily separated into sheep and goats. The result was – from a planning point of view – a mess, and the opportunity to provide wide open areas and major highways was doomed from the start.

To overcome this problem, it was necessary to create a second category of dwelling which would bring all the other areas in the overall plan within the Council's scope. Thus were born the – literally – 'grey' areas on the demolition map. To form the demolition areas into tidy tracts of land suitable for redevelopment, scores and scores more properties were simply shaded in. No reference was made to their fitness as houses, or improvements which may have been made within them. Their offence was not against hygiene but bureaucracy. They were in the way. The owners, who had felt secure in the good qualities of their homes as against some of their poorer neighbours', found to their horror that they had been lumped in together with them, in areas 'not fit for human habitation', 'condemned', and most cuttingly of all, as 'slums'.

There was a vital differential in the compensation to be offered. 'Pink' houses were considered effectively worthless as structures and their owners would be offered their site value only. Owners of 'grey' houses were to be offered the open-market value of the houses as they stood before demolition. Tenants of either sort were to be offered nothing at all, apart from an exceptional award for those considered to have 'significantly improved' their homes, which normally amounted to no more than shillings.

These orders extended the area begun by the Navy Inn Court Order, and amounted to a huge bite out of the area above the South Pier, the heart of the fishing community.

A huge shock rippled through Newlyn Town. Navy Inn Court's forthcoming destruction had been expected, but this was a very different matter. It included houses of every description, shops, cellars and stores, a vibrant part of the old village. Some of the houses were in very poor order, but some were clearly substantial granite cottages which had stood for two hundred years, and in the normal way would last hundreds more. Some properties were mass-owned by out of town landlords, but many were owned by their occupants, fishing families, who had borne generations of children within their walls. Some were mean overcrowded courts, but others were light and airy family homes. There seemed to be no logic to the decisions. The only thing they made clear was that nowhere could now consider itself safe from the threat of destruction.

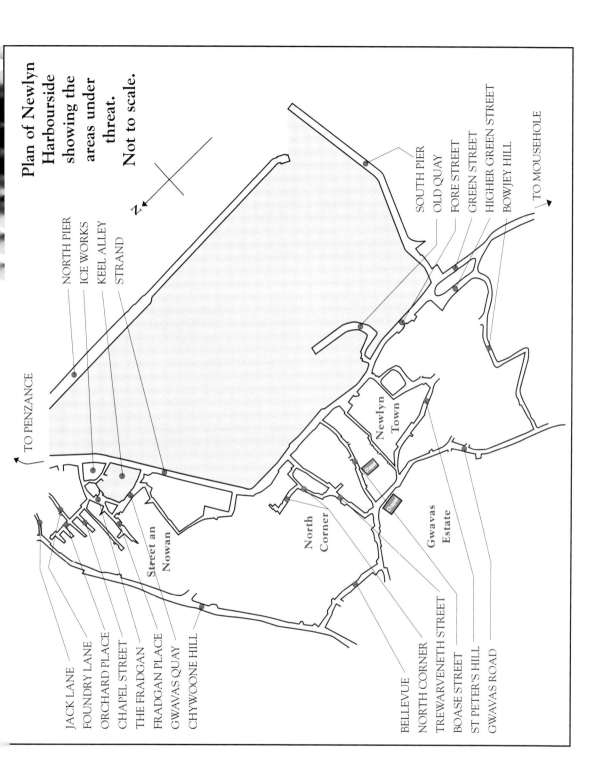

Plan of Newlyn
Harbourside
showing the
areas under
threat.
Not to scale.

N

TO PENZANCE

NORTH PIER
ICE WORKS
KEEL ALLEY
STRAND

SOUTH PIER
OLD QUAY
FORE STREET
GREEN STREET
HIGHER GREEN STREET
BOWJEY HILL

TO MOUSEHOLE

Newlyn
Town

Street an
Nowan

North
Corner

Gwavas
Estate

JACK LANE
FOUNDRY LANE
ORCHARD PLACE
CHAPEL STREET
THE FRADGAN
FRADGAN PLACE
GWAVAS QUAY
CHYWOONE HILL

BELLEVUE
NORTH CORNER
TREWARVENETH STREET
BOASE STREET
ST PETER'S HILL
GWAVAS ROAD

27

The process of the orders had to go through the requisite periods of notice, and allow time for appeal (by the owners), or if necessary a public enquiry. However resentful, the populace were not initially moved to disobedience of an official order. This was an era which obeyed the laws of God and Country as expressed by anyone in lawful authority, even the members of Penzance Council. The Council's right to act in accordance with the law was not challenged, at first.

But the sums of compensation offered for the dwellings in question certainly were. These could be, and were, immediately contested, in person, or with the help – for those who could afford it – of a solicitor.

Neighbourhood disputes have always been a significant source of business for Cornish solicitors, especially in such crowded areas as Newlyn, where the lack of space led to complications of ownership. 'Flying freehold' was common, where part of one property might lie above or beneath part of its neighbours', and some buildings might even belong in parts to three different people. At least one case came to light in Newlyn in which two different parties presented apparently legal deeds to the same property. Rights of way were a nightmare, mostly established by use and custom and not written down on any document. Even the rights of ownership were also often vague. The properties had very little value, and were rarely bought or sold. Owners knew what was theirs, and so did everyone else who needed to, but it might not be so easy to prove it to an official enquiry.

The effects of the orders were like a rock thrown into a beehive, a mass of activity and anxiety without focus, a mixture of fact and rumour, and an inevitable division into factions.

The most immediate protagonists were those with a vested financial interest, owner-occupiers or absent landlords, who joined battle at once on the compensation issue. They at least had a bone to chew upon which they did with a will.

Others were simply helpless and bewildered. The shock highlighted other divisions, which went to the root of their formerly orderly society. Newlyn was a fishing port, but fishing was changing. Its enormous success had been occasioned firstly by the export trade (mostly to Catholic countries who, by Papal decree, were prevented from eating anything other than fish on Fridays – hence the Pope's surprising popularity in an otherwise strictly Anglican community). The opening up of the railways had then provided a straight line to the home market in addition. The blockade of the First World War had provided a huge boost to the domestic market. However the increasing mechanisation of the industry and competition from abroad, as well as the eerie disappearance of large shoals of pilchards from Cornish coasts, had led to increasing poverty. The industry declined. Worse was to come as the international political situation deteriorated. In early 1937 the export of fish to one its main customers, Italy, was put under embargo, another devastating blow to the fishery.

Few of the younger and better educated generation looked to fishing as their living, having aspirations in cleaner, safer and better-paid occupations. Fishing was beginning to be seen as the way of the past, a trade practised by the 'old people'. Along with this schism went a mounting impatience with the old ways, and an increasing sensitivity regarding fishy smells and toilet arrangements. The teasing hurt the young, who did not want to be mocked by their Penzance contemporaries as old-fashioned, let alone primitive and disgusting.

A charming, if heavily posed early photograph, probably in the Fradgan
(Branwell Album, Penlee House Gallery and Museum Photographic Archive)

The subsequent struggle may have appeared as a straight fight between the outside forces of destruction and an embattled community united in the cause of conservation. Humanity is always more complex than that, and the hubbub aroused by the demolition orders included many notes of approval from within the village itself: yes, yes, tear it all down tomorrow and put up something decent instead.

But protest and dissent alike were confined to street corner level, and would probably have remained there until the steamroller of bureaucracy had rolled Newlyn flat, except that – higher up the hill – another regiment was gathering. These were not tired and inarticulate workers, used to having their wishes overborne by higher authorities. The artistic community were united as one in outrage. To most of them it was a matter of simple aesthetics. The uniform ranks of the new council houses were already appearing in the artists' own domain, and whatever their advantages in terms of light, space, gardens, and hygiene, their visual appeal was undeniably close to zero. The mess of courts and cottages by the water's edge on the other hand was an unending source of aesthetic delight as the light in the bay caught them this way and that, and the tiny streets provided perspective and charm.

To the artists the old houses represented the central character of the village, its soul. No 'improvement' could compensate for their loss, no matter how much their occupants might think differently. The idea of the harbour area being replaced with brutal modernism filled them with horror.

They looked for a single voice to express their opposition. They found one, across the road from the new Gwavas Estate, in Wheal Betsy, the fine house built by Thomas Gotch at the edge of a former mine. Phyllis, Marquise de Verdières, answered the call.

6 'OUR LITTLE WORLD'

Every year can be seen as a crucial hinge between the past and the future, but 1937 had many uniquely poignant features of a disappearing era.

The previous December, as Newlyn was assessing the threat to its existence, the King had stunned the nation by abdicating, leaving a shy and unprepared George VI to take on the burdens of state. 1937 was to see the new King crowned, a new Prime Minister, as Neville Chamberlain replaced Stanley Baldwin, and FD Roosevelt sworn in for a second term as American President.

In Europe the fascists were tightening their grip. Hitler and Mussolini held a huge joint rally in Berlin, and Von Ribbentrop, the German ambassador created a furore by greeting the new King George with a Nazi salute. The Spanish civil war was at its height, and in April a new horror was introduced to the world by the bombing of Guernica. A prison camp designed to house 'enemies of the state' was publicly and proudly opened by Himmler at Buchenwald. Further away, remote and sparsely reported, Japan invaded China and took Beijing with terrible bloodshed and atrocity.

Other events have a more contemporary ring. A royal commission was set up to solve the vexed problem of the division of Palestine. Australia protested at the flood of immigrants of 'the wrong kind' from southern Europe. A bomb exploded close to the royal entourage as they undertook a Coronation visit to Belfast. The first Motor Show took place at Earl's Court, Margot Fonteyn was dancing at Sadler's Wells and *The Hobbit*, a children's story by an unknown Oxford don JRR Tolkein

was quietly published. A GEC television set could be had for £50, although there was precious little to watch on it.

In the quiet obscurity of Newlyn the storm of controversy distilled onto the flamboyant form of the only daughter of Thomas and Caroline Gotch.

Tom Gotch and Caroline, née Yates, had been amongst the first wave of Newlyn artists, both arriving by way of the Paris ateliers, and both independently well off. Their daughter Phyllis was born on 6th September 1882 in France and the Gotches moved permanently to Newlyn – where they had met – when Phyllis was five. She never thought of herself as anything but a native of the village, she went to school there and absorbed a good deal of its culture, while remaining firmly part of the other-worldly community up the hill. She regarded the villagers as her equals, and probably never accepted the fact that her huge house, servants, dinner parties, dances and private income meant that the feeling could never be truly mutual.

She was spoilt, by her father in particular. His fascination with his only child bordered on the unhealthily obsessive, and she became the central figure of many of his more intense paintings, often in an impossibly idealised way. In *Alleluia* for example she is seen as the central figure in a choir of angelic young girls, surrounded by a golden architectural halo.

Phyllis' own nature was far from the solemn icon thus represented. She was originally a tomboy and then a rather wild young woman, ready at any moment to roll up the carpets at Wheal Betsy and dance the night away,

Phyllis Gotch, the young
Marquise in the role of 'Spirit
of April'
(Alan Shears Fine Art)

32

despite her father's disapproval. She had no discernible talent as a painter except as a cartoonist, but was interested in writing as well as singing, dancing and drama. In 1912 she moved to South Africa, where she fell passionately in love with a mining engineer called Ernest Doherty. They were married and had a child, Patsy, but Ernest caught the dreaded miners' disease phthisis and died in 1915. Broken hearted, Phyllis moved back to Wheal Betsy with her child.

She was too young and vital to be a widow for life, and was soon a favourite subject for local gossip and scandal. In the 1920s she delighted the gossips by undertaking a whirlwind romance with a French Marquis called André de Verdières. Rumour had it that she was attracted mostly by his title, and he mostly by her money, but in any case they were swiftly married. Mutual repentance followed soon after; his title was nominal; her money was no more than adequate; they parted after three years mostly filled with passionate recriminations. The only legacy she took from the Marquis was the one which had originally dazzled her, his title. She styled herself 'The Marquise de Verdières' for the rest of her life (although in Newlyn she was still mostly known, affectionately or otherwise, as 'Miss Phyllis').

She had actually abrogated the right to her title in 1936 when she was secretly married for a third time to a young law student called Jocelyn Bodilly. This caused further scandal when the marriage was revealed – he was 23 and she was thirty years older, although her marriage certificate baldly stated her age as '29'. However she had no intention of demoting herself to plain old Mrs Bodilly, and continued to style herself as a Marquise.

She was well-known throughout the village, an ostentatious character with strong opinions and plenty of articulate confidence with which to express them. She described herself as an author and did in fact publish a couple of books, one on her father's work. She also appears to have been well connected on some national magazines and newspapers, and was fascinated by what is now known as 'the media'. However, despite her airs and her long sojourns in London and abroad, her roots were in Newlyn with the people she had grown up amongst, and she never forgot it.

Phyllis was well acquainted with the changes in Newlyn from an early stage. She could hardly help this as the ground just across the road from the windows of Wheal Betsy had been torn up to lay out the lower terraces of the new estate. There must have been, as with many of the artistic community, a certain complexity as to motives. The natural order originally decreed that the villagers remained close to the harbourside down below, while the seekers of artistic inspiration sat on the hill above them. Now, suddenly, the villagers were to be arriving beside them, or in some cases leap-frogging above them. It was not to be borne.

The Marquise de Verdières sailed into battle.

On a parallel path went Geoffrey Garnier, an engraver and printmaker who had attended Stanhope Forbes' school and married a fellow student, Jill Blyth. They had lived since 1917 in an old house on Belle Vue called Orchard Cottage (which had been extended to include its neighbour in a long and rambling dwelling) and had a panoramic view of the areas to be devastated. Garnier was acknowledged as a Newlyn school painter, as well as a printmaker and engraver, but he was also a social leader. He had trained as an engineer, and in the Great War had served in

The desireable residences on Bowjey Hill on the left with their, then exotic, palm trees were cleared as slums
(Douglas Williams Collection)

the army, and when invalided out of that had joined the Royal Navy. He was well organised, used to the world of committees, and deeply interested and involved in the affairs of his adopted village, in which he was seen as a figure of some authority. As the alarm bells began to ring around the harbour, Garnier set up an emergency committee, the Newlyn and District Housing Advisory Committee, with himself as chairman, which the Marquise quickly joined.

Down at the sharp end, the role of spokesmen fell mainly to the Richards family. They were boat-owners with generations of fishing in their blood. Their house in Lower Green Street was amongst the first to be condemned although it was a fine granite dwelling and even had running water. The Williams, the Battens and the Harveys, large and complex families, were also soon involved in the grass-roots opposition. As many were to discover, their profession had not robbed them of the power of clear and persuasive speech. Their tradition of chapel-based rhetoric gave them an elegance in the use of language which was unfortunately not called upon often enough. They considered themselves uneducated, and preferred more learned men and women to do their talking for them.

Penzance Corporation was in no hurry to enact the Newlyn demolitions. The enlargement of the Borough had led to a vastly increased work-load and there were many other matters to consider. Treneere Estate was going forward, without the attendant controversy. The Corporation was particularly exercised with the preparations for the forthcoming Coronation, and other items on its agenda included a public toilet for Mousehole (which uniquely had to be combined with its storm defences), several applications for the increasingly popular 'Establishment of an Offensive Trade' (Fish and Chip Shop), and even the erection of a hoarding to advertise the nascent Minack Theatre. The Medical Officer of Health and his team continued to work their way through Newlyn from south to north, no longer appalled but determined to make a thorough job of it.

The final contract for building Gwavas Estate had been agreed – 242 houses and associated services and roads, for a total of £79,181 5s – with E Dennis and Sons of Camelford. It was not to be without its critics.

To begin with, the rent was far higher than the average rents around the harbour, sometimes double, over 8/- per week for the biggest houses. New bus services had been laid on, but there were soon complaints that the fares were higher than normal, with no choice of service. The bus was essential. Steep hills are not unusual in Newlyn, but the long slog up to the estate was for the able and unencumbered only, even when the weather was kind.

There were new regulations to observe, of which the most onerous was the prohibition of any kind of trade or business carried on from home. Many of the new residents had sidelines of one kind or another, needlework, mending, ironing, washing, and other domestic work as well as the variety of tasks associated with the fishing trade. The money was not great, but the double blow of higher rents and loss of additional income was discouraging to many who had originally resigned themselves willingly to the long climb.

There was also a limit to their desire for modernisation. The prospect of running water which did not have to be fetched, a proper bathroom, and the end of the evening run with the enamel bucket was a huge attraction. Some families divided on this single issue, the women more than willing to leave home and climb the hill to enjoy such bliss, while the men were determined that they would never leave the old village. But there was a ripple of dismay when they discovered that the new dwellings were to be fitted with gas cookers only. What about the Cornish Ranges?

Cornish Ranges were a forerunner of the Rayburn and Aga, a large stove kept burning most of the time, which not only cooked the dinner but dried the clothes, kept the houses aired, battled with the ubiquitous damp, and provided a warm place to park when coming in from the wet and cold. They may have been dirty, smoky and labour-intensive, but they were the focal point of most households. A gas stove was a chilly alternative, even though there were open coal fireplaces in the new parlours. The Council received a petition from 124 prospective residents demanding the Proper Thing: 124 new Cornish Ranges and a complete redesign of the kitchens to house them? The Council looked briefly at the costings and quickly rejected the request. Houses at Gwavas would continue to be

Trewarveneth Street 1931 – a favourite subject for photographers. A new coat of tarmac has covered the cobbles featured in earlier photographs
(Francis Frith, The Cornwall Centre, Redruth)

notoriously cold until the advent of central heating.

A different petition, the first of several protesting against the proposed demolitions in principle, was received by the Housing Committee at their meeting on 17th February 1937. It was condescendingly described in the minutes as 'purporting to have been signed by three hundred ratepayers', and was Duly Noted.

Things were warming up. After further representations, a special meeting was held between the Council and a few delegates from the fishing trade in April. The fishermen pointed out that, in their zeal for demolition and modernisation, the planners had never considered the practical impact on the port itself. All fishing boats had nets, which needed space to dry, mend and treat, and places conveniently close to the quays for storage. Fishing boats were small individual enterprises, each needed somewhere to put boxes and baskets, pots and floats, sails and oars and all the normal bits and pieces of their trade. Space was needed for repairs of boats and gear. Fish cellars would be required again if the pilchards came back. Gwavas was a country mile away up a steep hill, they pointed out, and in any case no provision whatever had been made there for storage or working space. It was a residential housing estate, pure and simple.

The difference between a model village and a working port seemed to have been lost on the Council's planners, and the fishermen's problems seemed to come as a surprise. However they reassured them that they would consider reinstatement of storage facilities to those – which they seemed to think exceptional cases – 'whose livelihood is connected to the fishing industry'. The main purpose of the deputation, whether the demolitions were necessary in principle, was held to be not within the remit of the meeting and no discussion of it was allowed.

But it was beginning to be discussed with vigour elsewhere. By early summer the first articles and letters were appearing in the local press, and one or two of the more rurally-minded national publications were taking notice of the forthcoming struggle between tradition and sanitation.

The Council's only response was the publication on 7th July of another large swathe of Compulsory Purchase Orders. Moving inexorably northwards, these included:

Fore St Order No 1
Gwavas Road
Boase St Order No1
Boase St Order No2
North Corner Order No1

together with another ancillary list of 'grey' areas in Green St, to the rear of the Red Lion, and up in The Meadow (above North Corner). Still in the firing line were Church St and Trewarveneth St, and then the trail of destruction could move down to Street-an-Nowan.

Those who had doubted before doubted no longer. The 1937 summer harbour sports day produced a programme with a scorching editorial, sounding a clear alarm. Entitled 'Newlyn in the Future' it cried:

There won't be any Newlyn in the future! … What is the scope of the measures designed? It is the clearing away of Newlyn Town, from North Corner to the southern end of Green St, from Gwavas Road, Myrtle Cottage, the top of St Peter's Hill, Ebeneezer Place right down to the water's edge, Church St, Boase St, Trewarveneth St –all to go. Houses on the Cliff – all to go: the little group of houses above the old quay – all to go: as well as the houses running down to the South Pier.

When this little work is done the turn of Street-an-Nowan is to come. ...The object of the Housing Act is presumably the health and well-being of those affected. And how is it proposed in our case to achieve this? By pulling down the whole town and moving a large part of its population....

And so on, in equally furious vein.

The most militant Newlyn 'Buccas' (locals), especially those who remembered the gunboats of 1896, were convinced that Penzance had seized the first opportunity since Newlyn had fallen within its power to finish the job off and root out its troublesome neighbours once and for all.

Geoffrey Garnier, who was partial to writing Cornish 'doggerel' contributed a poem beginning:

Our Urban Council oft we chide
and rue the day we chose 'em.
They make in secret dreadful plans
And see that no-one knows 'em

In the village carnival, Garnier's son Peter entered a float featuring a tottering shed bearing the name Austin Cottage (Mr Austin was Penzance's Town Clerk), bitterly entitled 'Homes Fit For Heroes'. The Marquise's contribution was a float comprising a group of beautifully dressed and immaculately turned-out village girls, entitled 'Angels From The Newlyn Slums'.

It was the word 'slum' almost as much as the impending destruction which aroused such passion. (It was not for another two years, after the full glare of national publicity, that a discreet memo went from the Town Clerk to the District Council asking them belatedly to substitute the words 'Clearance Areas' for 'Slum Clearance' in their reports.) Newlyn people at home and away seethed in fury at the description of their homes as slums, and their families as slum-dwellers. They knew well enough the hours of toil and the pride and love which had kept their homes decent despite poverty and loss. The slur fell on all alike, the rich and poor, the careful and the careless, the 'pink' and the 'grey'. Their homes were slums, fit only for tearing down and clearing away as if they had never been. And if Newlyn was a village of slums, they asked, who were the slum landlords who permitted such things? Often the friends, drinking companions and social equals of those who condemned them, over in Penzance.

Following their latest assault, the Council announced the date and venue of a major Public Inquiry to cope with the complaints which had been pouring into their offices. The complainants were invited to put their cases in person or via a solicitor, the first open forum for the expression of local feelings. It duly opened on the 20th July at St Johns Hall, Penzance.

Many of the protesters did not dispute the Compulsory Purchase Orders themselves, but concentrated on changing the designation of their houses from 'pink' to 'grey', from 'Site value only' to 'Open market value'. Financially the difference was worth fighting for. The smallest and meanest houses on St Peter's Hill had site values officially assessed as low as £5–£6. The site value of a good house was unlikely to exceed £50. For owner-

Chapel Street, Newlyn, October 1937
(Private Collection)

occupiers a 'pink' designation was the end. The compensation offered would not nearly allow them to buy anywhere else, and they would never again own a house.

This bore down especially heavily on the elderly and unsupported, whose only hope for solvency in their old age was the few pence they could pick up in odd jobs, and the fact that they had no rent to find – let alone the increased rents Gwavas would demand. Some had worked all their lives just to retain their homes, and the prospect of being thrown onto the charity of the parish through no fault of their own fuelled bitter resentment and despair.

Landlords also fought 'pink'ness, for different reasons and with more substantial backing. 'Open Market Value' was supposed to mean what it said, ie what a property would normally fetch in open market conditions, which should at least provide the opportunity to buy again. 'Pink' houses were worthless, and their investment would be lost.

The value of the 'grey' houses was another area of bitter disagreement. In theory the

A typical scene in the 'backside' the St Peters Hill area of Newlyn Town. A boy plays an accordian outside a cottage, while dogs, cats, children and babies listen
(West Cornwall Art Archive)

owners of these properties should have been able to buy properties of a similar value elsewhere. However the Open Market Value was assessed by Penzance's Borough Surveyor, hardly a disinterested party. The Borough would have to foot the bill in the end, and understandably its estimates were challenged and its motives impugned. Open market valuations as low as £12 6s 8d were soon being quoted in the press to prove the Council's bad faith. Once again the owners of such houses in poorer areas were destined to be priced out of the market altogether. This was desperately hard when it was agreed that there was nothing wrong with their houses in the first place. The 'grey' footprint had trampled over many sound and well-tended homes in its bureaucratic progress.

Newlyn solicitor Mr Hornbrook spoke for many of the complainants: 'The whole of Newlyn has been in a state of uncertainty for some time … it had been known that the Council had some plots hatching in their brains regarding Newlyn, but nobody knew exactly what they would be.' Later he was even more robust 'It has long been known that Penzance has had evil designs on Newlyn…' The integrity of the Borough Surveyor, Mr Latham, was not questioned, but the nature of his relationship with the

Council was perhaps best revealed by the following encounter, regarding the new layout following the demolition:

Hornbrook: When were the plans finished?

Latham: They were gradually being finished up to the time of the Inquiry.

Hornbrook: They have only been finished during the present week or last week?

Latham: Last week.

Hornbrook: The plans were not before the Council when they passed the clearance scheme?

Latham: The plans have never been before the Council at all.

Hornbrook: The Council might not accept your plans.

Latham: I do not think the Council will alter this plan materially….

Such airy confidence applied to a radical plan for a whole new village. In fact the plans for the new layout of the village never came to light, if they ever were actually finished.

The matter of proposed road-widening came up, since it condemned virtually all the houses by the quayside. Mr Latham favoured a radical approach when questioned by another solicitor, Mr Jewell Hill. Jewell Hill proposed that an 18ft roadway would be sufficient. But Mr Latham insisted on at least double that:

Latham: In my opinion it is absolutely necessary to have a 36ft road. If I had my way I should have a wider road to take three lanes of traffic as is the custom today on most of our roads.

Jewell Hill: The main traffic on this road is the Western National bus.

Latham: It has been suggested we should have a 60ft road there.

Jewell Hill: A 60ft road going through Mousehole?

Town Clerk: Round Mousehole.

Jewell Hill: If so there would be no Mousehole.

(Through the 1970s and 1980s, when eight or more fully laden trucks per hour were pounding through the narrows of Lower Green Street from Penlee Quarry, there were many who may have wished that Mr Latham had won the day, although now the pendulum has once again swung the other way).

The Enquiry wound on for five days. A few – very few – owners managed to present a scheme for improvements, often including knocking down or amalgamating neighbouring properties they also owned, which gained a reprieve from demolition. More managed to present a convincing case for the transfer of their properties to the 'grey' list. But mostly it was just a sad parade of disturbed and reproachful residents. They could not begin to accept that the houses they considered their own inalienable property could be snatched away at a bureaucratic whim. or condemned simply because they were nearby other condemned dwellings. Or that their housepround owners should suddenly be branded as 'slum' dwellers. They were stunned, indignant, furious.

An unnamed 'old lady' was represented who complained that she had lived in her house for 75 years without a day's illness. Mrs Bessie Strick was also widely quoted, saying that the last person to die in her Lower Green Street house had been a hundred-and-one. Another owner on St Peters Hill defended his home ' I have brought up four children without illness. There are six rooms in my house. It is a gentleman's house… '

The Council representatives were deaf. Every case, they promised, would be looked at on its merits but there would be no overall change in policy. The standards of ventilation and daylight were absolute and would be applied in every case, up to the furthest bedroom, without exception. The Town Clerk opined that 'including other areas, about 500 houses would have to go...'

The fieriest remarks came from Rev George Richards, on behalf of a Mrs Matthews, who was bringing up her three children in a perfectly decent house on St Peters Hill. He accused the Council of acting in a 'high-handed and arbitrary manner', forcing her to pay money in rent which she would otherwise have spent in educating her children. He described the new houses being built at Gwavas as 'among the monstrosities being condemned by architectural experts'.

It was the first statement of an issue which was to cloud the battleground forever after: the relative merits of the new houses against the old. In reality there was no conflict. Almost everyone accepted the provision of the new 'council' houses in Newlyn as they did everywhere else, though not all cared for their appearance or wished to live there. The question was not whether the new houses should be built or occupied, but whether so many of the old houses should fall in consequence.

But as time went on the two events became linked and sides were taken. Anyone protesting at the demolitions was seen as an opponent of the new estate. Anyone defending the new estate was seen as one of the vandals intent on the ruin of old Newlyn. All the later actions took place under this basic misapprehension, which has not completely disappeared even to this day.

Being a local affair the Enquiry was not without its quota of local spite. Mr Hornbrook apologised for the warmth of some of his remarks, but added that he was better able to criticise Penzance Council than Mr Jewell Hill, since his (Jewell Hill's) son was in fact a member of it. Another promising exchange was quickly cut short by the Inspector:

Hornbrook: I would not have you think these (the fishermen) are the sort of men to make a song and dance about their war service. There is a personal reason why I mention war service. It is that the Housing Committee ... has as its Chairman ......
Inspector: I don't think you need to go into that. I cannot go into personalities or local politics.
Town Clerk: (Hurriedly) I wish to say that the Chairman of the Housing Committee now was not the Chairman when the orders were made.

Having carried out its statutory duty Penzance Council then retired behind its walls once again, refusing to make any further comment. When the Marquise wrote on behalf of the Newlyn Housing Committee, requesting that they receive another delegation from the protesters, she was curtly turned down and was told rather mendaciously that the matter was now 'sub judice'. The Councillors lived to regret their arrogance, and their error in underestimating the Marquise. The next time they were to encounter her was across the chamber of the Council itself, of which she had become a duly elected member.

The close of the Public Enquiry signalled the open season in the press. The local papers, *The Cornishman* and the *Cornish Evening Tidings* had sided almost entirely with the Penzance view of the matter. Their eminent, if eccentric, owner Herbert Thomas (who wrote at least two broadsheet pages of his own opinions every week, including a long poem of his own on the occasion of the Coronation, not to mention a later piece entitled 'My

Planners in Fore Street ominously studying a map
(Alan Shears Fine Art)

Advice To Hitler') was one of a class and society with those pressing the reforms.

However other papers seized on the story, with a completely different attitude. The *Daily Telegraph* in particular took up Newlyn's case and weighed in with articles and letters – many from Cornish 'exiles' – lamenting the destruction of history and culture in favour of the blank face of modernism.

Newlyn was not alone in facing a bleak future. Mousehole was not then the tourists' favourite it is now, since as a working port it was full of the heavy atmosphere of fish, and living conditions there were if anything more primitive than in Newlyn. But it was still visually perfect, the beautifully proportioned harbour cradled in a circle of hills without a single jarring note of modernity, an archetypal Cornish fishing village already celebrated on many picture-postcards. Newlyn and Mousehole had not always got on, in fact several times their two communities had come to blows, but they were now united in adversity against their more powerful neighbour.

Plans for Mousehole never even reached the stage of formal inspection or division into

Fradgan Place, Newlyn 1931. This hidden area of Street-an-Nowan took a heavy toll of destruction, though some houses at the further end survive
(The Cornwall Centre, Redruth)

zones, let alone Compulsory Purchase Orders, but – together with the nearby village of Paul – it was all part of the same process, and the cold eye of sanitary disapproval had already been cast over it. In an unguarded moment the Borough Surveyor had mentioned that there were no major plans for demolitions in Mousehole, 'no more than about three hundred houses'. Presumably this was partly to accommodate the new 60ft road to nowhere in particular. Mousehole had no idea that anything on this scale was in the wind, but they could see what was happening on the other side of Penlee Point. They held a public meeting of alarmed residents and threw in their lot with the Newlyn Housing Committee to do what they could to spare their homes.

The Committee gave the press everything they had.

It was a gift of a story. All over the country some of the same scenes had been enacted, treasured parts of old cities and towns denigrated, condemned and pulled down, field after field broken in and seeded with an unsympathetic crop of mass council-housing. Nothing could be said in favour of the preservation of 'slums', or against the provision of sanitary housing, but there was resentment and nostalgia for the old ways lurking in many other places.

Newlyn and Mousehole were different. They were small, attractive, quaint, celebrated in art galleries all over the country, peopled by fishermen whose part in the Great War was still appreciated. These were simple country fisher-folk, national icons, *The Fishermen of England* of popular song, heart-wringing heroes of *A Hopeless Dawn*.

The *Daily Mirror*'s full page contribution was typical. 'Which would you rather see?' it cried, 'This …or This?' The first scene was in Chapel Street in Street-an-Nowan with washing on a line and a galvanised bucket … but nevertheless charming and reminiscent of many a Newlyn School painting. The second was a really quite attractive photograph of Chywoone Crescent in Gwavas, almost completed, in the sunshine with the sea in the background… but nevertheless sufficiently modern and geometric to make the necessary distinction. The *West Briton*, the *Western Evening Herald* and the *Evening Herald* all weighed in with similar photo-journalism, making unfavourable comparisons between the old and the new. *The Times* and *Daily Mail* ran several columns of serious comment, putting the fate of Newlyn on the breakfast tables of the nation. Stanhope Forbes, now nearly eighty, was called upon to comment and described the plans for his beloved village as a 'terrible blunder'. The popular Cornish author 'Q' – Sir Arthur Quiller-Couch – was also widely quoted in favour of conservation.

Feature writers were not averse to an autumn jaunt down to Cornwall. They arrived in numbers, and found a populace well-prepared to make the best of the bounty that visitors bring. The *Western Weekly News*' correspondent, for example, was accosted by an ex-sailor who proved a 'mine of information' and happily accompanied his benefactor all day and all evening. The sailor's nerve almost failed him when he was offered the reward of a meal in an expensive hotel, although 'his splendid appetite completely routed his class-conscious nervousness'.

The Newlyn Housing Committee decided to recruit a more professional witness than the journalists whose opinions could easily be disparaged. They commissioned Professor Stanley Adshead, Professor Emeritus of

Town Planning at London University, to give his opinion on the matter. After a two-day visit he set out his thoughts in a substantial article in the *Daily Telegraph*.

His statement read as admirable common sense, which might have saved much of the heartache and resentment which followed. He pointed out that the Housing Acts were framed to cope with city slums not rural villages such as Newlyn, and that architectural value could not be measured solely with a measuring rod and an inflexible set of rules. In Newlyn, which he obviously loved at first sight, 'pictures, viewpoints and incidents of special interest are to be found at every turn.' Regarding the widening of the Mousehole road, he said 'In providing improved roads for traffic, have we not in such cases mistaken the horse for the cart? Is it not conceivable that reduction in the size of the cart is better than improvement in the strength of the horse?' He concluded that the main lesson to be learned was that 'The Housing Acts need amending, to make special provision for dealing with cottages and villages possessing historic interest and peculiar charm.' It was incontrovertible, but no-one in a position of power was listening.

The position of the local MP, an emollient Conservative, Alec Beechman, was not enviable. On one hand he was bombarded by a vocal and distressed section of his constituency which had the ear and sympathy of the national press. On the other, his main political supporters were Penzance to the core, and he could hardly join forces against their legitimate actions, initiated as they were by his own Minister of Health. It was enough to make any politician squirm, which Beechman duly did, anxiously making caring noises about the fishermen's circumstances without actually condemning

the actions which had led to them. He convened a meeting of all representatives of all interested parties in the vain hope of some kind of consensus, without result.

The tide was running the other way. In Cornwall a unanimous opinion on any issue is almost an affront to nature, and inside Newlyn itself the stream of hostile outside comment finally produced a visible backlash.

The thrust of local protest had been against the destruction of old Newlyn, the forcible eviction of its residents and the financial hardship this would bring. However the tone of much of the national journalism took the aesthetic line, seeking to highlight the cause by making derogatory remarks about every aspect of Gwavas Estate, its architecture, appearance, layout and very existence. The build-up of outside condemnation grated on the poorest Newlyn tenants, who already considered Gwavas as their only life-line, a chance to better their lot and live in acceptable twentieth-century conditions. To many tenants of sub-standard property it seemed that a chorus of 'la-di-da' outsiders were telling them that they should stay in their charismatic, dank hovels and be grateful, rather than improving their lives by moving up to the 'monstrosities' on the hill.

They were fed up, and one of their number, identifying himself only as 'A Tenant', called into the offices of the *Cornish Evening Tidings* to give vent to his feelings. He described his domestic conditions graphically in a one-up-one-down cottage with himself, his wife and two boys sharing a bedroom, one washbasin between three houses and, inevitably, a brimming bucket at the end of every day. He noted that those who were most militant in defence of the

Gwavas Estate under construction October 1937
(Garnier Family Collection)

old village already lived up the hill, well away from it. He reckoned that 'eighty per cent of the working people of Newlyn welcome the building of the new houses, and are longing for the day when they will have a chance to live in them.'

'A Tenant' touched a nerve. The Newlyn Housing Committee hastened into print to assure the public that the saving of old Newlyn did not require the condemnation of Gwavas Estate, and that all those who wished to move there of their own free will should not hesitate to do so. But it was too late. A counter-insurgent group was forming, and the village was dividing into two camps. The pro-conservation group was larger, more articulate and more influential, but the 'modernisation' group was fiercer and more abrasive. The draft of their petition – written on behalf of the 'Younger Residents of Newlyn' was wildly provocative:

We, the young people of Newlyn, are no longer going to endure the filthy and insanitary conditions in which we live …

We say that Newlyn is no longer a fishing village – granted a few elderly men and a few out-of-date boats … they will soon disappear. The sons of these men are not going fishing. No sir, they are finding employment in Penzance and elsewhere.

We say that far too much has been made of a small grievance which the few fishermen might have, for after all they represent a very small minority in Newlyn. We cannot understand why the Council have allowed this propaganda to go unchecked...

Now that we, the younger people have opened the way, we hope the older ones will come out of their shells and speak for us.

Even individual families were divided. The women, who stayed at home and did all the domestic work, longed for any change which would ease their daily round. The men on the other hand wanted to find things just as they were, how they 'belonged', when they came home from sea.

But the inner voice of Newlyn was perhaps not heard in the anger of the young or in the polished statements of the Newlyn Housing Committee. At the end of September the *News Chronicle* published a large headline: 'Fisherwomen Pray For Their Condemned Homes – Service In Condemned Chapel' It appeared to be a piece of typical journalistic hyperbole, but was surprisingly true (except that the chapel itself was not under threat). A large congregation, not all of them women, had gathered for a special Service of Intercession in the Methodist chapel in beset Boase Street.

It was an occasion of almost tragic solemnity, including the singing of *Abide With Me*, *Eternal Father Strong to Save* and *Rock Of Ages*, and two minutes of silent prayer, a funeral service for a village. The address was given by a Penzance minister, Mr WG Pender, and captured the quality of the largely unspoken personal despair behind the ballyhoo:

Oh God, Thou knowest the men and women of this district are faced with the loss of their precious homes. Thou knowest how dear their homes are to them, and the years of toil and hardship and the loving sacrifice which have gone into their making, and what sacred associations are bound up in them.

They are the birth-places of their children, whose heritage they were to be. They are the refuge of the aged and of the widows who have no bread-winner to strive for them. Thou knowest that if we lose them, many amongst us must face earthly ruin. We beseech Thee to comfort and sustain us.

Our little world seems falling about us. We are bewildered and in sore distress. We beseech Thee in Thy infinite mercy that some means may be found to save these homes and preserve the villages of Newlyn and Mousehole for our own people. If this is not Thy will, we beseech Thee for the strength to put away all bitter thoughts and to face our lot with faith and fortitude...

A day or two later everyone was talking about the *Rosebud*.

Mrs Phyllis Bone and her dog at her door in Duke Street. Another car park stands here, although some of Duke Street has now been rebuilt to the traditional pattern
(Betty Johns)

7 THE SEA-ROAD TO LONDON

The idea did not come in an individual flash of inspiration. The brusque response to date made it clear that further petitions to the local authorities were a waste of time. The next step was to ride on the tide of popular support and take their case further and if possible to the top, to the Minister of Health himself. Buoyed up by the learned opinions of Professor Adshead, they would appeal for an exception to be made in order to preserve Newlyn's 'peculiar charms'. The Committee met to discuss ways and means.

In everyone's mind was the last great petition to the House of Commons, the Jarrow March of the previous year. This had begun in a small way, a delegation of desperate workers who resolved to walk every step of the way to the centre of government in order to draw attention to their unemployment, hardship

HANDS OFF NEWLYN!

IT IS SHEER VANDALISM

Local Authorities Challenged

Western Weekly News

'Fight the Good Fight', the *Rosebud* prepares to leave Newlyn (Garnier Family Collection)

and starvation. The press took up the cause, and by the time the column reached the capital it was miles long, and proudly flourished its union banners in the heart of the nation.

Another march was suggested, but no-one wanted an anti-climax, and, while Newlyn people were facing homelessness they were not actually starving. It was felt that they would suffer by comparison.

And then someone remembered that there was another way to the House of Commons, one uniquely appropriate to their cause, via the river. As soon as it was conceived, the idea caught on. A boat, a fishing boat, sailing from its home port directly into the Minister's parlour. Of course!

Press interest was rekindled at once. It had begun to slacken a little, after a fine innings. Even *The Times* had come to call:

'A visit to more than a dozen of the condemned cottages revealed them all as spotlessly clean and attractive as hard-working women with limited means can make them'. It was pointed out that for centuries Newlyn had produced outstandingly healthy

PRAYERS FOR NEWLYN HOUSES

Service of Intercession
UNIQUE OCCASION

SPECIAL PRAYER FOR DIVINE INTERVENTION

Cornish Evening Tidings

Fisherwomen Pray for Threatened Homes

Service in Condemned Chapel

Artists Join in Hymn Singing

News Chronicle

men and women. One fisherman claimed 'People don't die here; after a certain age we have to shoot them...'

Acres of newsprint, ranging from serious leading articles to further large photo spreads, in periodicals as diverse as *Country Life* and *Autocar*, had appeared. But when a pictorial feature article was published reporting that Newlyn housewives were baking special pasties as a thank-you to the Professor Emeritus, it was clear that the coverage was wearing a little thin.

On 4th October the *Daily Telegraph* broke the latest news, under the headline 'Petition Ship From Newlyn.'

Unknown to the *Daily Telegraph* several boats had been suggested and rejected, including the *Trevessa* which regularly made the journey to the East Coast. But brothers Billy and Cecil Richards, whose homes were directly threatened, insisted that their boat, the *Rosebud*, should be the one to go. The *Rosebud* was a typical Newlyn fishing boat, 50ft long, small but sturdy, of the type known as a 'long liner' 'herring drifter' or 'pilchard driver', depending on what fishing opportunities were afoot. Newlyn was her home port – she had

HEIRLOOMS SOLD TO SAVE HOMES

Village War on Clearance Scheme

Daily Sketch

been built there in 1919 by shipwrights Joseph Peake and Sons, from Cornish oak reputedly grown near Truro. She was constructed along the lines of the old coastal luggers, with a mizzen and the addition of a small petrol engine, and was quite at home in the extreme weather conditions to be found around Lands End.

The first snag, the most serious at the time, was the money. The journey was estimated at three to four days each way. She would need fuel and provisions for the journey there and back, and the time spent in London and, most pressing of all in a time of bare subsistence, neither the men nor the boat would be earning for nearly two weeks. The herring season was just beginning, and the income from it was crucial.

The Marquise came into her own. With the rest of the committee she organised a fund-raising drive, while at the same time milking the story for all it was worth to the national press. 'Heirlooms Sold To Save Homes!' howled the *Daily Sketch* – 'Keepsakes and jewels which have been handed down for generations are being sold in this tragic 'fight for survival'…. Shawls worn by the present generation's mothers, grandmothers, and great-grandmothers will be put up for auction…' The Marquise herself was interviewed, and demurely stoked the flames 'It is a tragic situation … their distress is pitiful … I love them and am helping all I can … they are ready to do anything to save their homes'.

It did not take very much of this sort of nonsense to start funds rolling into Newlyn from up-country, which added to the considerable sum already being subscribed locally.

There was soon enough to make the journey possible. More than enough would not have seemed proper. All the members of the proposed deputation were strict Cornish Methodists who worshipped at the Centenary Chapel on Gwavas Road. They were at particular pains to avoid the charge of luxury. They were (mostly) uncomfortable in the public eye, and sensitive above all to the accusation that they were going to London for some kind of pleasure jaunt. It was their sincere determination not to require more than the bare minimum in terms of supplies, accommodation or entertainment.

Another grass-roots petition had been planned by a group of local women before the

Newlyn Women Send Letter to Queen

News Chronicle

'LISTEN ENGLAND'

Women of Doomed Village Appeal To the Queen

Daily Sketch

Rosebud venture had surfaced. They had been charmed by the appearance and manner of the new Queen (later Queen Elizabeth, the Queen Mother) whose every aspect had been discussed and devoured in the press coverage of the Coronation. She was considered not only gracious but sympathetic, having suffered a bereavement herself in the Great War. The women elected to by-pass Parliament altogether, and appeal directly to royalty in a heartfelt (if grovelling) address:

We, your gracious Majesty's most humble and devoted servants, the women of Newlyn, whose precious homes are threatened, plead to the first lady in the land, our kind and beautiful Queen, who knows so well what the love of home means and who will understand above all others what the Celtic people feel about the soil on which their forefathers have dwelt for centuries…

It went on to describe their lot in more vernacular terms:

…the fishing industry is now looking up well… we love our homes dearly … we cannot afford to pay rent for the Council's houses…

It ended with wrenching emotion:
We are anxious that your Majesty shall know that the wives, widows and fatherless women who are writing this letter are all wearing the War medals won by our husbands and fathers. We are wearing them to show your Majesty all the honour and respect in our power, and to keep up our courage in venturing to write … for should your Majesty think right to plead for us, then the Empire itself would listen, and our sorrow and distress be heard.

It was despatched into the post office after a short prayer meeting around the War Memorial.

ARMADA OF 1 TO INVADE LONDON

Sunday Graphic

However the women's petition remained a local affair, not to compare with the story now unfolding in the national press, well summarised by the headline in the *Sunday Graphic* : 'Armada Of 1 To Invade London'

The Armada's crew had been chosen, after some delicate political manoeuvres. It was to be:

> CHB (Cecil) Richards, part owner
> W (Billy, or 'Swell') Richards, his brother, part owner and skipper
> JS (Jimmy Strick) Matthews, their brother-in-law

The *Rosebud* casts off (Richards Brothers Collection, Morrab Library Archive)

BG (Ben) Batten
JP (Sailor Joe) Harvey
W (Billy Bosun) Roberts, preacher
J (Jim) Simons
JH (Jan Enny) Tonkin
WH (William Henry) Williams,
  known to his family as 'Skinny'

'Miss Phyllis' had a hand in picking the crew, as in everything else, and was looking for talent suitable for the purpose, for – as Ben Batten remarked – 'while some were all right for Newlyn Cliff when it came to talking, there had to be one or two somewhere near the mark for London'. Her own talent for what is now the noble profession of public relations was uncanny. No doubt the bottles of holy water from Madron Well and the Jordan River were her idea also – if not she made sure that their presence was well known to the journalists.

The preparations reached a climax, the boat was prepared with what accommodation could be devised for the nine men, fuelled, filled with 'plenty of grub', lucky tokens, and the precious petition in a leather folder. Beechman had arranged for the petition to be received at the House of Commons on Wednesday 21st October. For comfort it would have been convenient for the expedition to set off on the 18th, but that was a Sunday and so of course out of the question.

Thus, early in the morning of the Monday 19th a hymn rang out, and the *Rosebud* sailed off into the morning sun.

The first leg was a familiar enough journey up the coast to Plymouth. The sunshine was quickly gone and the journey soon turned into a dour progress into a head sea and a cold drizzle, with the craggy headlands of Cornwall barely visible in the mist. The crew were

hoping to arrive in Plymouth by the late afternoon, but after a long and rough day's work they were glad to drop anchor in Sutton Pool at six o'clock. Their intention was to have their compasses immediately adjusted in Plymouth Sound and then press straight on. In the banal way in which ordinary circumstances can affect great enterprises, the pilot responsible for adjusting the compasses had unfortunately gone home by the time they arrived. They were therefore obliged to remain in Plymouth until he clocked on again at nine the next morning. It did however give them time to re-acquaint themselves with Mr Wilfred Hosking, a Plymouth accountant who had been rescued by the *Rosebud* the previous summer, when her crew found him adrift in a small sailing boat without food or water, and towed him to safety. He had asked them to call in on their way, and promised them a box of provisions to take with them.

The delay was a blow of some significance. At home the Committee had only just heard confirmation that the petition would be accepted by the Minister of Health in person, and he was expecting them at tea-time the following day. At a mean speed of no more than about seven knots, it was no longer a proposition for the *Rosebud* to be at Westminster Pier in time. It seemed that a golden opportunity was to pass them by, and that the petition would be received by a parliamentary minion, as they had always expected.

The next day the crew set off into much improved conditions. The morning mist swallowed them up and they were lost to the world. There was no radio contact, and no way of tracking the *Rosebud*'s progress, unless a coastguard or another vessel should catch sight of her. The press eagerly awaited her next appearance.

On board there was little to do, although they passed some of the time with a little light fishing. Sleeping was one priority – on a normal voyage the crew sleep in shifts, and on the overcrowded *Rosebud* there was no alternative. Apart from cooking and navigation, there was time for talking. They were a sober crew, literally and metaphorically, and the conversation may well have been more high-minded and philosophical than the equivalent today. They were on a mission, and they never took it less than seriously.

Unknown to them the surprisingly accommodating Minister been following their progress also via Lloyd's Register which was compiled by reports from coastguards and lighthouse-keepers. He had heard of their delay and had already readjusted his appointments in order to greet the Newlyn 'Pilgrims' – as some of the press were by now describing them – on the Thursday instead of the Wednesday. Their voyage may not have been observed but it was still front page copy. All the papers were giving it daily coverage, and when the next news of her reached shore it was literally printed in the 'Stop Press'.

'Petition Ship Grounds At Dover' said the dramatic headline in the *News Chronicle*. But it was not a story of disaster in the dreadful shifting sands of the Channel, but a short grounding in Dover harbour which had caused the excitement. The *Rosebud*'s crew were familiar with the coastal route to the east-coast fishing grounds but had no previous knowledge of the Thames Estuary. They called into Dover where the harbour-master was pleased to present the necessary charts to such celebrities. On the way out she lost the channel and stuck for a short while in the sandy harbour mud, but the oaken hull was not troubled by such trifles, and as the tide flooded she soon broke free.

The tireless Marquise was already in London, stirring up all the attention she could create, with considerable success. At her prompting, a special BBC Radio debate had been set up for 10pm that evening, between herself and Robert Thomas, Mayor of Penzance. However, early in the evening a series of panicky telephone calls between the BBC, the Town Clerk of Penzance and the Ministry of Health led to the sudden withdrawal of the Mayor. Since no-one else was willing to put the case for Penzance, the BBC decided that the Marquise could not be allowed to debate with herself – although she was more than willing to do so – and cancelled the programme.

In the darkness most of the *Rosebud*'s crew were on deck all night, 'picking up different lights' and keeping themselves safe on their unfamiliar course. They passed Sheerness at 2.15am, Southend before 4.00, and Gravesend by 7.40. Just as light was dawning *Rosebud* entered the mouth of the Thames itself, and started the long haul up the river, against the tide.

If they had expected to slip quietly to their destination, they were soon confounded.

Their voyage had gained in the telling, and the reports of sightings had whetted the public appetite further. Perhaps not all the shipping they passed was aware of their identity, let alone their purpose, but the sight of the relatively tiny fishing boat picking its way between the mass of commercial shipping, the huge docks, and the wharves with their forest of cranes, was astonishing enough. Every vessel they passed hooted or whistled to honour their passage, and the sensation spread up-river before them. Crewmen, tug-boatmen and dockers waved and called as they went by,

Rosebud nears the Houses of Parliament (Richards Brothers Collection, Morrab Library Archive)

Cecil Richards, part-owner of the *Rosebud* who became the spokesman for the fishermen (Private Collection)

while the bemused Newlyn men waved back. As they pushed further into the heart of London, the public also were lining the river hoping for a glimpse of them, cheering when they were spotted. The press joined in the triumphant progress. Seen from the shore, *Rosebud* looked little and quaint, but the press corps had chartered a river-boat to follow her on her last lap. From water level she was a more imposing sight, and a small police launch preceded her port bow, making her seem larger by comparison. The cameramen waited for the perfect moment.

And it came. Following just astern, the massed photographers went into action as soon as the Houses of Parliament came into view. The whole crew of PZ 87 were on deck, gazing in wonder at their reception, waving or raising their fists in response. The police launch led the way, a standing policeman occasionally leaning across to call out advice. An archetypal double-decker bus stood on Westminster Bridge. The hands of Big Ben stood at five past eleven. The little fishing-boat steamed on towards its destiny, bearing the hopes of its people, as bold and brave as any vessel that ever sailed the Thames. The cameramen, realising that they were looking at a truly classic photograph, squeezed and squeezed....

It was by far the biggest news in England that day. The *Evening Standard*, The *Daily Mirror*, the *Daily Sketch* and most of the rest had an image fit to fill half a broadsheet page, and to stir the heart of a seafaring nation with a soft spot for an underdog. The pictures filtered down to the local press, had another round in the periodicals, and appeared ever afterwards when any development in the story occurred. The contrast of the stately outline of the Houses of Parliament and the graceful lines and perky stern of the little vessel which had come there in supplication was a picture worth more than a thousand words. It surpassed the most extravagant hopes of the Committee who had sent it there, lodged in the heart and the memory, and still has the power to move and amaze us. The *Rosebud* chugged on up-river into history.

Westminster Pier was a scene of bedlam as she tied up, thronged with people; friends, relatives, officials, Cornish 'exiles' moved to tears by the sight of a Newlyn vessel in their midst, the Marquise and other members of the committee, Jack Hitchins, a member of Penzance Council, who also happened to be best friend of Cecil Richards, Mr R Walpole, Chairman of the London Cornish Association, and press galore. Well-wishers poured onto the *Rosebud*'s decks filling them 'from stem to stern', while hundreds more called down their good wishes from above.

Alec Beechman MP waited on the steps, aware of the fact that he was within earshot of his political masters, and – calling for silence – began at once to sell the *Rosebud*'s crew back down the river:

I am delighted, to welcome the fishermen of Newlyn who are arriving in such a romantic manner, because it is well that the citizens of London should be conscious of the existence of these fishermen who, I am sorry to say, are encountering very great difficulties in making a livelihood.

The fishermen of West Cornwall did service in the war which could not have been done by others. They manned the 'Q' ships and minesweepers, and it is a nation's duty to see that these men are preserved – I use the word 'preserved' because I know from personal experience that the inshore fishermen of West Cornwall are fast being extinguished.

He had finished, with not a word about the evictions and demolitions or the forthcoming devastation of Newlyn, which had been the whole purpose of their journey. The pressmen were closing their notebooks. Billy 'Bosun' Roberts could stand it no longer. He roared out to the assembled national press:

The Cornish boys are here to fight for their homes! – a tremendous cheer went up – *The homes that their fathers and mothers lived in. They want to level the place and we shall not let them! He that does right shall come right, and we shall win!*

Billy 'Bosun' was preacher by trade, and his peroration was greeted with huge applause. It was reported in most of the papers along with Beechman's address.

The tired men of Newlyn were escorted off their vessel. The Marquise took the stage, telling the crowd that the men had sacrificed a great deal of time and money to make their pilgrimage, and pointing out that the public were welcome to make a donation towards their costs. The opportunity to 'wish' on the

Alec Beechman, MP for St Ives shows the Newlyn fishermen the sights of London
(Richards Brothers Collection, Morrab Library Archive)

bottle of Jordan water was also mentioned, and a proposed charge of sixpence for a (necessarily brief) conducted tour of the *Rosebud* completed the commercial side of the proceedings.

The crew climbed onto the steps of London, where most of them had never set foot before. Billy 'Bosun' checked Big Ben by his giant pocket-watch as it struck twelve and found it ten minutes adrift by his reckoning, which delighted the press even further. The party made a triumphant progress to a restaurant in Victoria where lunch awaited them, courtesy of the London Cornish Association. After that they had the opportunity to rest, before Beechman gave them a short tour of the Houses of Parliament. Soon enough it was time for tea, and time to Meet the Minister.

8 INTO THE PARLOUR

It was a short walk through the rain to the Ministry of Health on Whitehall, but long enough for nerves to do their work. The men had brought no changes of clothes, but had carefully pinned on all their wartime medals for the occasion. They knew they would be received, and that the Minister had put off other appointments in order to see them. But would tea mean a carefully balanced china cup and saucer, a few minutes self-conscious conversation and a quick retreat? What more would a sophisticated minister of the crown want with a bunch of barely-educated fishermen?

WHITEHALL IS STARTLED AS FISHERMEN ARRIVE

Cornish Evening Tidings

They went into the building, accompanied by Beechman. Some of the ministry staff who were not expecting the visit gazed in astonishment as the Newlyn crew came through the marble hallway and were led down the corridors of power in their hats and jerkins and jackets, followed by the faint but distinctive aroma of fish. They went deep into the building until they were outside Room 30, the Minister's private study. What met their eyes was the biggest surprise yet of this remarkable day. But they did not know

their man, and like others before and after, found themselves amazed by the diligence and imagination of the mild-looking gentleman who was waiting to greet them, Sir Kingsley Wood.

In many ways Sir Howard Kingsley Wood was the regular Tory grandee he appeared to be. Aged 56, rather short and a little stout with thick round glasses and white hair, he seemed a typical old-school politician at the summit of his career. His rise to high office had been steady. In his private life he was a lawyer who had worked his way up from being a prize-winning student to owning his own firm, Kingsley Wood, Williams & Co, Solicitors of Walbrook and Euston Square, of which he was senior partner. His public service had started on London County Council and led him to the chairmanship of the London Pension Authority and the London Insurance Committee, as well as serving as a JP in Brighton. Wood was knighted in 1919, the year the *Rosebud* was built. A year earlier he had entered Parliament as Conservative member for Woolwich East. He soon made his mark, and was involved in the setting up of the post-war Ministry of Health which he later led. His first cabinet post was as Postmaster General, which he held for four years. He was highly sociable, a member of the Constitutional, the Carlton and the Athenaeum Clubs, and was known to be close to his leader, Neville Chamberlain.

However he was not as stuffy as he may have appeared. His mother was one of a family of actors, a relative of Sarah Siddons, and he had married the daughter of an artist. While Postmaster General, he had been heavily involved in what would now be called media

Cecil Richards has tea with health minister Sir Kingsley Wood. Alec Beechman MP watches on (Private Collection)

campaigning but was then called, without shame, propaganda. Indeed he later chaired a government committee devoted specifically to the uses of propaganda. He understood the effect of newspaper advertising and eye-catching posters, but was also a pioneer of the Public Service Film, now recognised as an art form of its own. His campaigns promoted the Post Office (which he defended against privatisation), and in particular encouraged mass use of the post-war novelty, the telephone. More than most of his generation he was acutely aware of the power of an image. He had appreciated the symbolism of the *Rosebud*'s mission and had given a good

deal of thought to how it should be handled.

He decided that, instead of simply reiterating his former ministerial decisions and sending his Cornish petitioners on their way, he would turn their embassy to his advantage. They had achieved a notable propaganda coup, and he was determined at least to even the score.

Sir Kingsley was notably thorough in all he did, and took the trouble to inquire what kind of tea would be appropriate for his guests. Cornish tea, he discovered, was not a matter of china crockery and cucumber sandwiches taken at five, but a far more substantial matter taken at four. He had sent to Cornwall, to a supplier in Looe, for pasties, saffron cake, clotted cream, scones and the other constituents of a 'proper job' sit-down tea. Thus the *Rosebud*'s crew were greeted, to their amazement, with a conference table covered with a white table-cloth and laden with the best of Cornish fare, together with a large silver tea service.

Pasties and Cream in Ministerial Sanctum

Cornish Evening Tidings

There was immediately another new experience for them. The fishermen were seated, and then – instead of tucking in – took a passive role in a twenty-minute photo call with a large bank of waiting photographers, in three relays. The Minister repeatedly held the teapot and poured tea for his visitors for the benefit of the cameras. It was thoroughly stage-managed and the symbolism was clear. The humble men of the sea in their medals, were personally attended and even served by the knighted Minister of State. One all.

Sir Kingsley had greeted all the men with a firm handshake and a warm welcome. Unlike the tea ceremony, the hand-over of the petition was very briefly recorded. 'Right' said Wood smoothly as he received it, 'This shall have my most earnest attention. Now come and set-to.' Having thus finesssed any possible discussion of the matter at hand, he indicated the tea table. The petitioners picked up the cue, anxious to show that they knew their manners, and the subject of housing in Newlyn formed no part of the teatime conversation.

There were many other things to talk about. Wood was a man of genuinely wide interests and enjoyed discussing the details of their voyage, the state of fishing in general, their war-time experiences, and other similar matters. He asked them whether they fished on Sundays, and was informed that they were convinced Wesleyans and would never do such a thing. Wood probably knew this already, but it was something they had in common. Wood's father Arthur had been a Wesleyan minister, and he himself was treasurer of Wesley's Chapel in City Road, which he invited the whole crew to attend if they were still in London on Sunday.

Gradually the embarrassment of the Cornishmen fell away and, under the influence of Wood's powerful charm, they were soon chatting like old friends. Despite their hearty lunch, the crew had no difficulty in doing justice to the table, and the tea flew past in a convivial atmosphere in front of the coal fire which Wood had thoughtfully provided. At length it was over and Beechman rose to make a formal vote of thanks. Billy Roberts was not to be outdone in the exchange of compliments. 'When I put my hand into that of Sir Kingsley Wood, I knew his was the hand of a friend and a strong man. Sir Kingsley would have made a great fisherman.' The Minister courteously replied that Mr Roberts would have made a great diplomat. Later Ben Batten said 'I would trust my life to him in a hurricane.'

They left Whitehall in a state of euphoria. But still the most extraordinary day in their lives was not over. They were taken by taxi to a Gaumont cinema near Sloane Square, where a Movietone News film of their arrival that morning was shown on the big screen, to their astonishment and delight. When it was over the house lights went up and the manager called them onto the stage. The Marquise was there to make an introductory speech, and they stood there shyly to receive the enthusiastic applause of the packed audience. It was almost too much to believe.

Despite many more comfortable offers most of the crew elected to spend the night back aboard their boat. Their day had begun uncertainly off the dark coast of Kent and ended in absolute triumph. The men, their vessel and their mission were the talking point of the capital.

LONDON CHEERS CORNISH FISHERMEN

The Star

9 LONDON WEEKEND

Their petition rested in the Minister's office:

We the undersigned inhabitants of Newlyn and district wish to protest respectfully and strongly against the wholesale destruction of our village.

This ruthless appropriation of private property involves, in most cases, the loss of a lifetime's savings and the means of livelihood.

We claim that no such drastic action has been permitted in any other part of the country. We earnestly beg your very serious consideration of this disaster with which we are confronted.

It was signed by 1093 Newlyn inhabitants.

Very soon it was to be joined by a counter-petition from the militant group of younger Newlyn families, claiming around four hundred names. They urged the Minister instead to allow them to move to more hygienic accommodation as soon as possible, and to proceed with the destruction of old Newlyn as soon as he liked.

No doubt pondering with a sigh on the Cornish character, the Minister put them both away for his measured consideration in due course. He must have thought the public interest would decline fairly sharply now that the voyage was over. But even his wide experience had not included the like of Phyllis Gotch. As soon as the *Rosebud* was properly organised as a tourist attraction the Marquise was working on the next stage of the campaign. The men had done their stuff. It was the women's turn.

There had been talk of taking the women's petition to London personally instead of

NEWLYN WOMEN IN LONDON

All-Night Journey To Join Rosebud Crew

Wolverhampton Echo

posting it, but at the time practical objections had won the day. Now it seemed the Newlyn protesters could do no wrong. Money was coming in nicely, which had been the main stumbling block, and the eyes of the nation were upon them. The Marquise decided to send for reinforcements, and cabled an imperious telegram back home summoning all those women involved in the petition who could to drop whatever they were doing and catch the night train to London. Although not stated, the clear implication was that since the men had been received at the Houses of Parliament, the women might be similarly welcome at Buckingham Palace – not for tea, perhaps, but certainly to present their suit to royalty in person.

The women in question were thrown into a panic. All the afternoon, while their menfolk were scoffing saffron cake and scones with cream with the Minister, their wives and families were deciding who should make up the party, who would look after whom while they were away, and – not least – what they should wear. The Marquise had been specific. With her innate genius for newspaper appeal, she had instructed the women to dress in their everyday Newlyn clothes, knowing that this was how the country would wish to picture them. But that was too hard a choice. They would not be able to take a change of clothes each, and to present themselves to the London press, let alone royalty, in less than their best was an impossible sacrifice to ask. Off went the weekday pinnies, out came the chapel clothes in shades of black. The hair was brushed and combed and put into order, and crowned with a suitably solemn hat.

They arrived at the station with time to spare, and were photographed on the steps of the train. Soon the hour struck nine, and the excited party were off on their uncomfortable ten-hour journey. By the time they reached Paddington the next morning their spirits were still high, and they were ravenously hungry. They had a large breakfast at the station, then piled into taxis for the journey to the river.

Hugs and Kisses on Pier

Manchester Evening News

The press had of course been alerted and were waiting by the *Rosebud* for their arrival. 'Here they come' shouted one of the crew, as the women cantered towards the steps. They rushed down to the decks to board the boat they had seen off in the quiet morning just four days earlier. Now they too joined the ranks of national celebrities. Mesdames Matthews, Harvey, Batten, Tonkin, together with two widows, Mrs Wakfer and Bessie Cotton made up the party, and, since Cecil Richards' wife was unwell, his daughter Hilda had also been included.

The wives and widows were photographed and interviewed, but it was Hilda who caught the eye of the press. She was a pretty, gauche seventeen-year-old, a shorthand typist employed by – although it was not mentioned by anyone – Penzance Council. The press fell upon her, describing her as 'rosy-cheeked', and 'hazel-eyed' and quoting her every word. These mostly consisted of disparaging remarks about the London she had never seen before. She had been expecting a river full of huge docks and great ships as her father had described, and a city filled with shops and people. The elegant river flowing between state buildings and the quiet heart of Westminster on a wet Saturday morning was not up to her imaginings, and she said so.

The skies cleared, and the combined party set off for another guided tour with Alec Beechman, filling the terrace of the Houses of Parliament from side to side. They split up to go sight-seeing for a while, and then the women took over, stating their intention to 'man' the *Rosebud* while the men went off to further the cause. But most of the men stayed on the boat, around which a sizeable queue had formed. Some of the visitors called merely from curiosity, to see the famous boat and hear the Cornish accents. They were impressed above all at how small and vulnerable a vessel she seemed to be, and were silenced when the fishermen told tales of what conditions they regularly endured aboard her.

A large number of the visitors had no need to be told, they were Cornish exiles, full of homesick emotion at the sight of such a familiar object in such an unlikely setting. Some were from Mounts Bay, some recognised men and women on board they had not seen for years, or met other friends in the crowd, and they enjoyed the comfort all Cornish people feel when meeting each other far from home. The visitors had to be conducted around in parties, the Marquise once more supervising the lucky wishes and the tanners.

But the summons to the palace had not come.

IT'S THEIR HOMES THEY WANT

Manchester Evening News

In the evening most of the party were guests of the London Cornish Association who invited them for a pasty supper and a suitably sober Whist Drive. Then the men went back to their crowded berth, and the women to an even more crowded one, sharing a single large room in the guesthouse of a Cornish exile in Sussex Gardens. Luckily no-one made a point of comparing their overcrowded choice of London quarters with the overcrowded conditions at home which were at the heart of the controversy, or the light-hearted coverage might have descended into actual farce.

On Sunday the womens' choice of clothing was fully justified when they followed Sir

Kingsley Wood's suggestion and attended Wesley's Chapel, for many of them the high point of their visit. Afterwards they laid a small wreath at the recently-installed Cenotaph, and then resumed their duties with the Sunday afternoon crowds around the *Rosebud*. But there was still no royal command. One more day away from home and their domestic duties, one more day in such close proximity with even the best of friends would be enough, and the women determined to return home on Tuesday morning, Queen or no Queen.

Their visit, apart from prolonging the excited press coverage, had not been a great success. They had had no moment to compare with tea at the ministry, and if the press had been sparingly patronising with the brave fishermen, they could hardly restrain themselves with the women, or with the reunited Cornish colony which had sprung up beside the quay. 'Colour' pieces abounded, along the lines of : 'Mary Jane (Matthews) is a fine buxom woman, thrilled by her first visit to London….' etc. A *Times* leader summed up the slightly quizzical response of London to the Cornish rustics :

The ways of the 'delectable Duchy' have a rich complexity denied to the single- stranded English. To compare the crew of the Rosebud *to hunger marchers …is to rob the cruise of the* Rosebud *of a very subtle, delicate, elusive but unmistakable flavour of the comic. Yet to mention the comic is to be made intensely aware of the wide difference between the* Bellman's *crew that went snark-hunting and these very earnest and capable men of the sea who know precisely what they want and shrewdly choose a very likely way to get it. The simple Englishman, suspecting yet admiring the stage-management of the whole thing and the adroit use of the correct 'properties', saffron cake and the rest, and gratefully gathering his* Rosebud

while he may, falls back with a sigh of comfort on the word 'Cornish'. These are Cornishmen – which explains everything, or (just as good), leaves everything inexplicable.

The delicate flavour of the comic would have been elusive indeed to the congregation at the service of intercession at Boase Street Chapel, but London (then as now) saw Cornish affairs from the far end of the telescope. In fact the stage management had mostly been on the English side. But it was better to be thought amusing than ignored, as the Marquise knew well. She was to be lampooned in her turn as the Newlyn women returned home, having seen no more of the Queen than the railings of Buckingham Palace. A short but cutting piece of doggerel appeared in the little-known publication the *Newlyn Annual*, by an anonymous author:

Miss Phyllis, Miss Phyllis she went to town
To save our homes from tumbling down
And who do you think she took wi' she?
Why dear little Renee and six of we.

Miss Phyllis had said we'd got to go
But why we went we've yet to know
The Queen she said would talk wi' she
And dear little Renee and six of we.

What e'er we saw, where e'er we'd been
We saw no King and we saw no Queen
And what we think is just that She
Had never heard nothing of none of we

We went by night on the London train
And after a week were back again
But dear little Renee remained wi' she
And that left only the six of we.

'Dear Little Renee' was Renee Matthews, the Marquise's housekeeper (later Renee Nash, a local poet in her own right). She was not amused and pointed out in the press that she had not actually been amongst the party, and that moreover the unknown author could obviously not count to seven.

Punch also resorted to verse to commemorate the event. On October 27th it printed a poem called *Newlyn v Penzance*, which told the basic story while finding as many contrived rhymes for each town as possible, ending:

Each to his own. Penzance may sleep,
Swaddled in palms and sanitation,
So Newlyn (and the country) keep
The modest homes that make a nation;
If not, both reason and romance
(If England study either school in)
Tell us we might not miss Penzance
But cannot do away with Newlyn.

Not all took the matter so lightly. On the Monday night Sir Leslie Hore-Belisha, MP for Devonport and Secretary of State for War gave a dinner for his colleagues of the National Liberal Party (conjoined to the Conservatives), at which Alec Beechman was invited to give an account of the *Rosebud's* visit. The elite company were filled with sympathy and admiration. The Chancellor of the Exchequer suggested that it might be unwise to visit the boat and pay their sixpences along with the general public, but they all wished to show their support in a practical way and so after dinner they passed the hat. Into it went contributions from Sir John Simon (Chancellor of the Exchequer), Leslie Burgin (Minister of Transport), Geoffrey Shakespeare (Parliamentary Secretary to the Admiralty), Robert Bernays (Parliamentary Secretary to the Ministry of Health), and MPs George Lambert and Sir Harry Fildes.

The last Cornish invasion of London had been in 1497 when a rebellious throng was cut to pieces by Henry VII's army at Blackheath. But they did not penetrate nearly as deeply into the heart of government as the 1937 'Armada of One'.

The women went home on Tuesday bright and early, while the men prepared to spend a last day in the capital. The previous day they had met Sir Dingle Foot, MP for Dundee whose family had long association with Cornish Liberals. His father, Sir Isaac had stood unsuccessfully against Beechman in the recent election.

Poor weather on Tuesday prevented the *Rosebud's* departure, but allowed the crew to join the crowds watching the procession to the State Opening of Parliament. It was the closest any of them would come to the royal family. Lord Runciman, President of the Board of Trade, came to Westminster Pier the next morning to see them off – he was well known to them having been Beechman's predecessor as MP for St Ives. Beechman also came to the send-off, and even he had come some way off the fence following the triumphant weekend. 'We all hope,' he said daringly 'that Penzance Council, in making good the conditions in Newlyn, will find it possible to carry through its plans without undue hardship or causing serious injury to Newlyn's charm.' This time even Billy 'Bosun' felt no need to add to his sentiments.

At about 9.40 the little boat untied from her now familiar berth and slipped away down the Thames. There was no hullabaloo, just a few waves from the dock workers on the way, and the occasional toot on a siren. The *Rosebud's* nine days' wonder was nearly over. As she made her way towards the Channel, the Minister of Health was being questioned on the Newlyn issue in Parliament, during the debate on the King's Speech. As before he reserved his position pending his deliberations. The voyage back to Cornwall was easier than the voyage up, involving only one stop at Dover. The crew met a hard north-wester and rough seas off the Eddystone, but as for all returning Cornish people, the pull of home proved stronger the closer they came, so they 'put a hard face on it' and carried on. At about quarter to seven on the Saturday morning, while it was still dark, she quietly came back through the 'gaps' into her native port, and tied up between two other fishing boats. She had been supposed to call into Plymouth to wire her expected time of arrival, so that a reception committee could see her in, but the crew had had enough of celebrity and crowds. They longed to return to a quieter, more private life, and took mischievous pleasure in returning to their own homes unexpectedly before most people were about. Their greeting was no less warm for being out of the public eye. They gave themselves the rest of the day off, and the regular crew prepared to take the *Rosebud* back to sea the next day, to resume her interrupted career as a fishing boat.

The only one who did not seek repose in the quiet life of home was the Marquise. The local municipal elections in which she was a candidate were to take place on 2nd November, and she threw herself at once into strenuous campaigning.

Penzance Borough Council, the body the Marquise was anxious to join, were in a state of siege. From a well-meaning if heavy-handed instrument of domestic hygiene, they had become nationally branded as uncaring vandals bent on the destruction of traditional charm and beauty. It was the perceived injustice of Penzance Borough Council which had propelled the *Rosebud* towards the House of Commons, and the whole country knew it.

Despite the scrum of journalists seeking a quote with which to balance their coverage, the councillors remained resolutely silent. Only the Mayor, Robert Thomas, briefly broke the embargo, complaining that despite publicity to the contrary, they were not 'The Pirates of Penzance', and that they were dealing as carefully as possible with a problem foisted upon them by the requirements of the state. But the rest refused to engage in public debate, and despite the affront to their integrity, determined to stick to their task. Their most eloquent response to the national outcry had been published on 20th October, while the *Rosebud* was wearing along the south coast of England on her quest of mercy:

Compulsory Purchase Orders:
Gwavas Road
Boase Street Order No 1
Trewarveneth Street Order No 1
Trewarveneth Street Order No 2
North Corner Order No 1

The shadow was spreading northwards. As a diplomatic response, it was plain enough.

The Marquise canvassed on Newlyn issues, the amelioration of the housing cull, the provision of proper mains water and sewage, the retention of local schools (a cruel blow had been struck when Newlyn's only secondary school had just been scheduled for closure, the children to be sent to – where else but – Penzance), and 'extravagant expenditure on swimming pools, fancy gardens and the like'. On 2nd November her manifesto won the day, and she shared the two seats of the South Ward with Mr E Tonkin, a fellow believer (and Newlyn property owner), while the retiring member who had sided with Penzance, Mr T Tonkin, was unseated.

Apart from the political melée, there was a nervous silence in Newlyn. Their futures waited judgement. Before the Minister of Health, as they saw it, were two choices: either endorse the actions of Penzance and continue the devastation of the village; or dictate a policy change, rescind the previous orders, make the necessary improvements and restrict the demolitions to those strictly necessary. Go ahead, or go back. Newlyn or Penzance. A dilemma.

The trade of politics hates dilemmas, especially when either course is sure to be greeted with controversy. Any politician will usually avoid a situation where sides have to be taken, and Sir Kingsley Wood was not just any politician, but a senior minister and a highly experienced old fox. Given the choice between supporting his own policies and aiding the fishermen who had won the country's heart, he did not take long to ponder his next step. It was, of course, sideways.

The first news hit the news stands the day after the local elections, while the newly-elected members were still expressing their public thanks. A special edition of the *Cornish Evening Tidings* was rushed out with the headline in the biggest point size the hot-metal print could manage:

'NEWLYN SAVED'

To the careful reader, the rest of the article would have scarcely justified the banner headline. There was reference to 'only a small block of houses too bad to be saved', but there were also references to 'preserving frontages', and an ominous passage in which the Minister welcomed the assurances that the council were 'prepared to re-house the fishermen and older people near the harbour'. He referred continuously to preserving the 'amenities' and 'providing suitable accommodation'. The fishermen and older people did not want to be re-housed, and it was their homes rather than their frontages or their amenities for which they were fighting. But the headline stood tall in black and white; and the small print could wait.

NEWLYN GETS RESPITE, REVELS ALL NIGHT

Boat Pilgrims Saved 94 Homes

Daily Mail

The next day the national press confirmed it. The *Daily Mail* headlined 'NEWLYN GETS RESPITE, REVELS ALL NIGHT, (an unlikely scenario) BOAT PILGRIMS SAVED 94 HOMES' As the good news spread, according to the report, 'the villagers started all-night revels and cries of delight re-echoed through the streets as they danced together' Other papers chimed in 'Rosebud Did Not Sail In Vain', 'Reprieve For Newlyn Cottages', or the *Daily Herald*'s more circumspect: '*Rosebud*'s Cruise Saves Some Homes Of Fishermen'.

NEWLYN SAFE FROM VANDALISM

No Destruction Of Picturesque

FISHING INDUSTRY NOT FORGOTTEN

Penzance Town Clerk Replies To Critics

Western Morning News

Some indeed. The tally of houses already condemned for demolition (not including the order issued during the *Rosebud*'s voyage) was 157. Of these Sir Kingsley had actually reprieved 23, mostly vehement protesters who owned their own houses in 'grey' areas. Although a small proportion, 23 houses reprieved meant 23 households unburdened from the threat of homelessness and loss of their life-savings. On its own it was sufficient justification for the efforts of Cecil Richards and his crew. But the remainder of the 94 homes in his report were not saved at all. Of these 54 were to be transferred from the 'pink' list to the 'grey', thus granting their owners the cold consolation of 'market value' when they fell. The last 17 were tenanted houses, still 'pink', still condemned, for which the tenants were to be offered small sums for 'significant improvements'.

The rest of the Minister's emphasis had been on the quality of the rebuilding, the participation of the Council for the Preservation of Rural England, and the preservation of the facades of the houses around the harbour. He was confident that Penzance Council desired to deal with the matter 'in a sympathetic way'.

And that was it. The Minister bowed out, amid a flurry of headlines acclaiming the saving of Newlyn, all praising his role in dealing with the men of the *Rosebud*. The national press bowed out also, having participated in a charming story with a picturesque climax and a happy ending, and of no further interest. And Penzance Council had only got as far as North Corner in Newlyn Town. They had half a village to deal with yet, and virtually carte blanche to do as they wished.

Around the harbour the horrible news began to sink in. The original interpretation seemed to imply that only a few really rank houses would fall, a proposition no-one disagreed with. But the idea that the rest of the village would be preserved and reconditioned was curtly slapped down in a statement the next day by Penzance Town Clerk Mr Austin, saying that the Minister had granted the Council 'substantially all it had asked for.'

It was greeted with bewilderment and dismay. A reporter from the *News Chronicle* door-

HAVE NEWLYN HOUSES BEEN SAVED?

Local Fishermen Bewildered

WHAT DID HEALTH MINISTER MEAN?

Two Interpretations Of Decision

Western Morning News

73

The axe swings – the end of the Navy Inn, 1939
(West Penwith Archive)

stepped Cecil Richards with the news that his own house in Lower Green Street was not one of the lucky twenty-three, and was still to be destroyed. What was his reaction? His reaction for a few moments was a dignified silence. He then said 'I feel it would not be wise to say a lot now.' Then added defiantly 'But I can tell you that we fishermen still have a lot of fight left.'

The next day, to the *Western Morning News* he stated 'A member of Newlyn Housing Committee called me a pessimist when I declined to hang out our flag as a sign of victory. As a fisherman I know there is a big difference between seeing a shoal of fish and actually getting it into the nets. I am inclined to think now that we have not very much to rejoice about in this decision.'

It was not only the loss of their own and their neighbours' houses which bore down upon the *Rosebud*'s crew, but the sense of personal disillusion. They had met the Minister, shaken his hand and looked him in the eye, the Minister who had treated them as equals, the Minister who 'would have made a great fisherman', whom they 'would have trusted their lives to in a hurricane.' Now the door of the Ministry was closed to them once more, judgement had been passed, and there was no further avenue of appeal. Bitterness made them silent. The matter fell out of the local press also, and, in spite of Richards' words, the appetite for resistance on a large scale was no longer there. Instead there remained the fierce determination that when it came to the last, they would not be parted from their homes by any means except physical force.

The big picture fractured into hundreds of smaller ones, every house its own battlefield.

Penzance's victory had had its price. The airy schemes for broad-brush modernisation were no more. The eyes of the country had focussed on their secluded byway and there was no chance that any hidden agenda could slip through for lack of scrutiny. The press slept, but once a story has been established it is easy to revive, and another scandal in the land of the *Rosebud* would be sure of widespread coverage.

There was no longer any question of bossing their smaller neighbour into doing their bidding unnoticed. Every fall of every stone would have to have justification sufficient to stand up to legal challenge. Proposals for 30ft, let alone 60ft roads were buried under oceans of paper, never to re-surface. The protesters had not gained their objective, but they had ripped away the comfort of obscurity, and the councillors of Penzance were fully aware of where public sympathy lay. Through familiarity and through their disagreeable mutual history, they had regarded old Newlyn only as an unhygienic anachronism, of no intrinsic value. Now they had to swallow the popular verdict on how short-sighted they had been: 'We might not miss Penzance, but could not do away with Newlyn…'

It stung.

Sir Kingsley had held off from confirmation of the Compulsory Purchase Orders until he had seen evidence of consultation with the CPRE and other bodies, and looked at the plans. By Christmas he was able to write to the Council that he was 'pleased to note that the elevations and designs of the houses are so in keeping with the character of Newlyn' (where he had, incidentally, never set foot) and saw no advantage in withholding confirmation of the orders before him.

Meanwhile the first tenants had already moved into Gwavas, mostly from Navy Inn Court and Factory Row. Before Christmas of 1937 Miss Welsh had already fallen down the stairs of 1 Chywoone Place, due to a defective stair rail, and started a lively correspondence on the matter of compensation which was destined to last for most of the war. For many it was their first Christmas with toilets and hot water, and this engendered a fondness for the estate which still endures in their generation. Gwavas was completed in May 1938, although ancillary works continued until July 1939.

In January 1938 one of the 'other bodies' specified by the Minister had their promised consultation with the Council, the representatives of the Newlyn fishermen. Amongst them were *Rosebud* veterans Cecil Richards, WH Williams, 'Sailor Joe' Harvey, as well as Jimmy Matthews' wife, the 'buxom' Mary Jane. Oddly placed amongst those on the other side of the table was the recently installed South Ward Councillor, the Marquise de Verdières. The issues were mainly those discussed already, but the fishermen asked if they could not retain the freehold of the houses once rebuilt. They were told it was out of the question. It was clearly a paper exercise, and the Housing Chairman, Alderman Trenwith brought the meeting to a close after less than two hours, promising again that each case would be dealt with individually. The fishermen went away, grimly promising that they would certainly be doing so.

The Council had started nibbling at the other parts of their enlarged borough, identifying a few houses in Sheffield and Paul for demolition, but the job at Newlyn was not yet

Bowjey Hill – all gone – compare with picture on page 34.
Three men walk down from Gwavas past the wall and gateway which are all that remain
(West Penwith Archive)

complete. However on 11th February 1938 the last major Order was issued, taking the last step northwards into Street-an-Nowan, completing the shadow which now lay over the whole village. As well as further orders concerning Fore Street, Coopers Court, Boase Street, Trewarveneth Street and North Corner, there was fresh ground:

Wesley Place
The Fradgan Order No 1
The Fradgan Order No2
Chywoone Hill
Duke Street No 1
Duke Street No 2
Jack Lane
Dolphin Court

as well as most of Farmers Meadow and other pockets of land and cottages on the lower ground.

Once again some of these – especially Duke Street – were in poor order, but many were sound. Some had tenants anxious to better themselves by joining those already installed at Gwavas, a number of whom had regarded the voyage of the *Rosebud* as an unwarranted interference in Street-an-Nowan's aspirations by uppish Newlyn Towners. But many were owner occupied, loved and cherished, with the life savings of their families wrapped up in them.

Penzance had finished the first phase of their mighty task, but already had their hands full with phase two. All the objectors who could took the Council at its word and engaged it in one-to-one disputes. Though they had won the right to demolition in principle, in every case the Council had to go through a similar procedure to a legal purchase. Even today the purchase of some 350 houses from individual owners would be a large undertaking, but as previously mentioned, the identification of the properties, the frequent absence of deeds, the establishment of the myriad rights of support and rights of way, the odd pockets of land which were unclaimed, unknown or belonged to someone else altogether were a fertile source of disagreement and delay. And then there was the whole field of negotiations over compensation.

The element generally lacking in the process was the goodwill of the vendor. Any excuse would do for another round of enquiries, each delayed as long as possible. Production of documents could take months, until threats made it unavoidable. Papers were 'lost'. Relatives were abroad and correspondence took time. For example Mr Kliskey who owned several cottages in North Corner was at the time prospecting for gold in California, and an exchange of letters therefore involved journeys by train, boat, train, and packhorse to an ever-changing campsite. Neither Mr Kliskey nor any of the other absent owners had foreseen the prospect of forcible legal proceedings during their absence, and deeply resented the need to deal with it.

The law's delays bought Newlyn time, but no real hope of changing the eventual outcome. They might all have to go in the end, but they would not go quietly.

However there was one course of action open to Penzance which did not have to wait for legal completion. It started in 1937, become a trickle by January of 1938, and by May it had reached a flood. Street by street, square by square, the men from the Council came to call, and nailed eviction notices to the doors of houses, cottages and lofts. Gwavas was almost complete and the new houses had to be tenanted within a certain period or much of the grant aid to the Council might be forfeit. While the final reckoning of compensation for the owners still had to be hammered out and the houses formally transacted, the dwellings were now legally endorsed as being 'Unfit for Human Occupation', and it was the Council's right and duty to rehouse their occupants at the first possible opportunity. They were given seven days to move themselves and their belongings to their allocated addresses at the top of the hill.

There was no attempt to re-unite the communities in their new setting. Families were moved according to administrative convenience, and found themselves side by side with unfamiliar faces, people from other streets or courts, up or down the pecking order, sometimes almost complete strangers since Newlyn Towers were mixed up willy-nilly with those from Street-an-Nowan. Much travelling and visiting took place through the windy avenues as former neighbours located each other and kept in touch while having no more than nodding acquaintance with their new next-doors. It was easier in the estate to keep oneself to oneself. There were walls made of block, and gardens with fences and their own front paths.

Many loaded their carts and went rejoicing up the hill, determined never to come back. They had no business with the harbour and all they wanted was a decent home for themselves and their families. They closed the door on their damp, dingy hovels for the last time and left without regrets, to go up into the sunshine to a new life.

For others it was a grief too deep for words. Their 'little world' had indeed ended, the close-knit society of shared joy and hardship, the gossip and laughter at the water shoots, the mutual care and support, the sound of the boats coming into port and the footsteps of the men coming home, the chatter around the peaceful harbour in the evening, the enmeshed world of cousins, aunts, grannies, in-laws, the children running everywhere, always under the eye of friends or family, the smell of the bakehouses, the little shops and tiny enterprises, the warmth and security of an ancient and organic community. Instead they were destined for a suburban enclave of self-contained residences, with no meeting-places, no sense of mutual need, no history, no soul.

They parted in tears with those who were to stay behind.

They took every opportunity to return to their home village, to meet each other in the old places and keep hold of the past, but it was not the same. It was their home no longer. Many families had remained behind, and many were not even under threat, but in 1938 some of the heart went out of Newlyn, and never came back.

Some refused point-blank to be moved, and waited for the enforcement notices, promptly delivered a week later, followed soon afterwards by the bailiffs. But not many. Working-class people have to learn to be pragmatic, and tenants without homes of their own had to choose between the new houses or none at all. With old people and children to care for, there was really no choice, and so they went up the hill with the rest to make the best of it.

The council men went swiftly from place to place, padlocking doors and boarding up windows. Living cottages became blank-faced, derelict ghosts. Whole squares and courts were left empty and silent.

It was a huge cull from the small community around the harbour. Twenty-nine households were cleared in 1937, a hundred and eighty-six in 1938, forty-two in 1939, and two as late as 1940. By the time Mrs Blackburn's family of three were removed from Gwithiel Gwavas in May 1940, just under a thousand men, women and children had been evicted from their native village.

Much of old Newlyn, so recently 'saved', lay naked and defenceless, waiting only for the wrecking gangs to come and do their work.

11 HITLER TO THE RESCUE

But of course the little world was part of a wider and deeply troubled continent. The very names of the years 1937, 1938 and 1939 now toll like bells warning of inevitable catastrophe, although there was always hope at the time that war might be averted.

Preparations were however being made on the home front. Gas masks, bomb shelters, air raid drills, the Home Guard, all became part of everyday life. The government looked to its domestic resources. Gardens had to be dug over, and flowers exchanged for vegetables. Ornamental metal was appropriated and melted down for scrap. The housing stock too was to be put to full use. Grand houses were requisitioned for use as administrative headquarters and hospitals. Smaller ones in the country would soon be required to house the flood of evacuees from the vulnerable cities.

Already beset by the flood of legal work necessary before the derelict houses in Newlyn could be demolished and redeveloped, Penzance Borough Council was made aware that emergency accommodation might soon be required in its area, and was required to make an audit of what was available. While they could hardly turn around and offer evacuees dwellings which they themselves had so recently condemned as uninhabitable slums, they had to admit – however unwillingly – to the possession of half a village of empty property.

It was already a thorn in their side. Apart from the ongoing legal attrition, complaints were pouring in about the empty property.

A southerly view of the scene on p76 – the site seems to have been gravelled prior to the building of Bowjey Court Flats
(Morrab Library Archive)

Much of it was empty no longer. Rats and mice had lost no time in moving in, and the Council's boarding-up was no more than a challenge for children looking for 'dens'. Some enterprising folk had even re-opened cottages and let them to new tenants, regardless of whether they owned the cottages themselves or not.

At Gwavas too not all was peace and light. The first winter had been a revelation, with the reality of gales and long uphill walks in the rain balancing the bliss of the bathrooms. The houses had been built to pre-set patterns without consideration of the weather, and there were complaints that the chimneys would not 'draw' in certain winds, leaving the houses smoke-filled and cold. Gas was expensive and the pressure variable. Some houses were prone to flooding in storms. The bus fares were still a problem. There were sadder developments too, complaints at the gangs of children which had formed and passed the time by throwing stones at the windows of the houses still unoccupied, or making a nuisance of themselves in neighbouring farms. There was little enough for them to do on the hill, and the old village was too far away for them to go unsupervised. Before the move they would have dispersed into the streets around the harbour, never far from a watchful relative, with the sea, the beaches and the boats to play with. No-one would have got away with throwing stones at other people's property there. But things were different.

Some of the displaced Newlyn tenants had turned down the new estate and had made other provision for themselves. Parts of Gwavas were offered to those on waiting lists from Mousehole and Penzance.

Treneere estate in Penzance was completed in November 1939, with no apparent fuss at all.

Just after the outbreak of war a circular went out from the Ministry of Health, authorising local authorities to postpone works due under the Housing Acts. All action on the Newlyn clearances, apart from the evictions, was suspended. Threatened with destruction by its nearest neighbour, Newlyn was reprieved by its country's bitterest enemy. Hitler had come to the rescue.

Newlyn's character changed considerably during the war. There was, for example, no night fishing. The whole of the daily catch was bought by the government and allocated according to its priorities. The Navy moved in and appropriated the South Pier, and several fishing boats were enlisted for purposes much removed from fishing, spying, ferrying special agents, intelligence and other covert work. A few bombs fell, but mostly in the harbour doing little damage. Apart from the fishermen and the Navy the village emptied of men and became quieter than ever.

The empty houses continued to rot. At a meeting of the Housing Committee in May 1940 those present discussed what was to be done with the houses in the clearance areas. They resolved to take no action.

However, although the vacant properties were not considered fit for occupation by evacuees from up-country, it occurred to the emergency authorities that they might be good enough for foreigners. A steady influx of French and Belgian fishermen had fled the German advance with their families, some bringing their boats with them. More were joining their fellows, and a colony of Belgians was forming in Newlyn. Unofficially they were offered the best of the Newlyn 'slums' as temporary accommodation, and they accepted with alacrity. The Ministry of Health was not amused, and demanded that they be found alternative accommodation forthwith, but by then other houses were being opened up to cope with the second wave of English evacuees. In the showdown between the Ministry of Health and the emergency billeting authorities, those pursuing the war effort were bound to win. Penzance Council were therefore set to task, making emergency improvements to the houses they had resolved to flatten, including the plumbing and sewaging they had previously stated to be impossible. Former villagers visiting their old haunts from Gwavas were amazed and disconcerted to find their old homes opened up, renovated, and filled with Londoners and, in particular, 'Belgiques'. To many it was the final insult.

Or almost. In June 1941 the local Home Guard applied to the Council for permission to use the still empty houses and lofts of St Peters Square, once bustling homes for large families of Battens, Blewetts, Harrys and Thomas's and others, for a hand grenade throwing demonstration. It was turned down.

Of the 350 dwellings condemned in the Council's original orders, only 58 had fallen by 1940, and two of those were due to fire. A further round of demolition, in particular Dolphin Court, took place in 1943. For some reason the quiet backwater of North Corner was pursued with exceptional vigour and eleven out of the nineteen cottages originally condemned were down by 1945, though Dod Procter's cottage and studio were spared. The law continued to grind also at Farmers Meadow, most of which belonged to the Hutchens Trust, a charity based at Paul, and most of the houses were finally brought down after a long legal tussle in 1948. But after a war containing so much destruction, the appetite for deliberate wholesale clearance of viable property had gone. There were

piecemeal demolitions in between, tooth-like gaps appearing in familiar streets, but no further widespread demolitions until 1951, when large derelict areas of St Peters Hill, Place and Square, as well as a number of houses in Lower Green Street, Church Street, Fore Street and Gwavas Road were finally lowered, with little public outcry. The destruction of a block of houses at the Fradgan was the last large-scale clearance operation in 1955. Many of the owner-occupiers who stood their ground had their reward, and lived to see the hated orders withdrawn and the threat to their homes disappear, including Cecil Richards, whose house still stands, and was still occupied by his daughter Hilda at the time of writing.

There was – and remains, despite the passage of time – a residue of anger regarding the sums of compensation offered by the Council. Even granting their best intentions, Penzance Council acquired a great many houses and large tracts of land at literally knock-down prices. People were seriously impoverished if not actually ruined, and their lives changed for ever. Some householders had no option but to accept the compensation offered, and then had to watch bitterly when, after the war, the Council disposed of many of the buildings they had appropriated but failed to destroy, at vastly higher prices.

By the time Penzance Borough Council gave way in its turn to the even larger Penwith District Council in 1974, one hundred and thirty of the dwellings considered unfit for human habitation in 1937 were still standing and happily occupied. Some years later most of them were included in the Newlyn Conservation Area by the same body, preserved in perpetuity from destruction or even alteration by the same authorities which once condemned them.

12 AFTERWORD

The village of Newlyn remains much as it was, a village devoted to the fishing industry, which is in just as precarious a state as it was in 1937. It still sets its clocks by the rise and fall of the tide and never really sleeps. The surviving 'slums' coiled around the harbour are for the most part beautifully restored and kept, although now (as then) beyond the reach of most local families, who are once more having to take their chances as tenants. A few are holiday cottages, but Newlyn's bustle and noise and faint but still present smell of fish have preserved it from the worst of the prettification which has overtaken other ports. Newlyn is still a working port, occasionally rough and rowdy, but very much alive.

The grand scheme devised by Penzance Council never transpired in any form. The rebuilding to designs approved by Sir Kingsley, the monstrous road, the model areas of residential housing and green spaces, none of these can be discerned in the village today. It remains a pleasant mess to look at, ancient and modern jumbled up with no apparent plan, an organic growth as before. Most of the areas which were cleared were never built on, being left derelict for some time then claimed for a purpose not envisaged in the nineteen-thirties, car parking. The greatest damage was done where the scheme began, in the south part of Newlyn Town, and the impact is increasingly less apparent further north, while large parts of Street-an-Nowan show virtually no signs of the conflict.

Gwavas Estate also continues to thrive. The population settled down and came to terms with their new environment. Apart from the discovery of a brothel in Chywoone Crescent – a clear breach of the clause forbidding the carrying on of a trade or business – the war left it unscathed, and a new generation grew up there. Through the fifties and sixties its reputation gradually declined as Penzance Council, neighbourly as ever, used it as a destination for their problem families. The houses continued to be very cold, and began to show the signs of poor insulation by becoming musty and damp. The grim warning given by an old lady at the 1937 Public Inquiry that her condemned house would continue to be going strong when the new houses were falling down began to look like a reality. Eventually the new District Council carried out a huge and expensive renovation and insulation project which cost many times the original £79,181 5s, and Gwavas began to revive. Today it is increasingly aware of its own identity and has a new sense of pride. Given the choice offered by the *Daily Mirror* between 'This...or this?', most people would still opt for the traditional granite cottages with roses round the door, but the rift between old and new was always more of an outside perception, and Newlyn still needs not either, but both.

The Marquise's third husband, Jocelyn Bodilly, became an eminent lawyer and later a high court judge. The couple moved to London and later to the Solomon Islands and eventually to Hong Kong, where Phyllis died in 1963. Geoffrey Garnier stayed in the village, continuing to oversee its activities from Orchard Cottage until he too died in 1970.

Sir Kingsley Wood was prevented by the war from relaxing into his well-earned retirement. On the contrary he made the transition from Chamberlain's government – where he had been moved in 1938 to the crucial post of Air

Minister – to Churchill's. Churchill recognised the steel behind the charm and in 1940 made him his Chancellor of the Exchequer. Among his first tasks was the procurement of armaments from the United States, nervelessly signing contracts for huge sums which his country clearly could not honour, until the Lend-Lease agreement relieved the financial pressure. After the early crises, he put his able mind to the reform of the tax laws. He died suddenly in September 1943 on the day he was due to present his proposals for PAYE, the system which still survives him, to Parliament. He left no children.

Of the *Rosebud*'s crew, only William Henry Williams died during the war, sadly drowned in a fishing accident in his native Mounts Bay. Cecil Richards' experience and character were rewarded when he was made Chief Fisheries Officer for Cornwall. He had the final satisfaction of dying in the cottage where he had been born, the one missing from the Minister's list for reprieve in 1937.

Did their voyage really achieve anything?

Most definitely. Although the Minister declined to rescind his original intentions, the huge wave of publicity which followed their efforts put a full stop to the more extravagant notions of the Penzance visionaries. They had assumed the absolute right to remodel Newlyn as they thought best, and were firmly reminded that the village was not just their territory but part of the national heritage and consciousness. After the *Rosebud* everyone had to watch their step and play by the rules. There are still people in Penzance who insist that they never intended to do anything else, but that was certainly not the perception at the time. PAS Pool's *History of Penzance* dismisses the whole matter in a short paragraph, while admitting it caused a little 'misunderstanding' in Newlyn. The misunderstanding caused many losses, but Newlyn did not become the thirties fantasy of block and concrete which could so easily have risen from the wreckage.

Another village has even more reason to thank the *Rosebud*. Chastened by the stiff resistance put up by Newlyn, Penzance Council did not have the heart to begin the whole process again in Mousehole. The Medical Officer of Health and his merry men did not even set foot in the village, and the proposal for the giant highway and the demolition of 'around three hundred houses' was never taken up. Instead almost every dwelling in Mousehole is more or less as it was, improved beyond recognition from the damp, dark poverty of the past, but still intact. The courts, the fish lofts, the tiny cottages all remain, and there is no better way of picturing pre-war Newlyn than by exploring the perfectly preserved alleyways and buildings of its near neighbour.

The *Rosebud* herself saw military service as a patrol vessel, being renamed the *Musk Rose* and sailing out of Belfast. She was sold after the war to two Thomas brothers who re-named her the *Cynthia Yvonne* after two of their children. She continued to fish out of Newlyn, and was known as a lucky and successful boat. Eventually she was sold on again, used for cray-fishing, and eventually bought by a consortium who intended to use her as a tender in an ambitious attempt to locate and raise the wreck of the *Titanic*. The enterprise came to grief and the dilapidated vessel was left unattended to rot on Lelant Saltings, to the distress of those who knew of her former history. Local children who played on other abandoned vessels in Lelant were warned off the hulk of the *Rosebud* by the older fishermen. Even in decline she was

The *Rosebud* now called the *Cynthia Yvonne*
(Douglas Williams Collection)

granted a measure of respect. A number of serious attempts were made to raise funds to rescue and restore her, but the sums involved were always too great.

In 1987 a ceremony was held to celebrate the fiftieth anniversary of her voyage. On 20th October a slate plaque was unveiled on the side of the 'Mission', the Royal National Mission to Deep Sea Fishermen, briefly telling the story and listing the names of the crew. It was erected by the recently formed Newlyn Association and unveiled by sons and daughters of the crew.

It was not to be the last commemoration. In the early 1990s the Newlyn Association conceived a more ambitious plan and gained a lease from Penwith District Council (whose ownership naturally dated from 1938) of a patch of derelict land at the top of the car park which had formerly been the busy St Peters Square. There they proposed to lay out a memorial garden to the *Rosebud*, and after three years' hard work, the money was raised and spent, and the gardens were opened by Hilda Richards.

In 2000, the site of a former pair of cottages in the 1930s battleground of Lower Green Street was finally restored to the use for which it had always been intended, and Penwith Housing Association completed a block of four flats for rent to local families. It is named Rosebud Court.

As for the vessel herself, she remained a hulk while various schemes for her restoration came to nothing. At last she was considered to have deteriorated so far as to be a hazard to other boat users, and her remaining spars and planking were pulled up onto the car park at Dynamite Quay in Lelant. A small notice appeared in *The Cornishman*, inviting all those who wished to take a piece of her home as a souvenir to turn up and help themselves. It was not the most dignified end, but many people availed themselves of the opportunity, and some used the timber to make models in her memory. The last physical remains of the *Rosebud* are therefore scattered around the community, with parts of her in many a store and workshop (including my own).

However, for the *Rosebud* the time will always be five past eleven on the 22nd of October; the year 1937; the place the muddy waters of the Thames below the Houses of Parliament; and her mission the saving of her native port and the relief of its people. She has earned her place amongst the immortals.

THE APPENDICES

These two lists, *Register of Houses In Clearance Areas* and *Register of Individual Houses Not Repairable* a taken from the records of Penzance Corporation.

They reflect the story itself. The first list starts in clean and tidy order but becomes more chaotic, and t second list, made further into the battle, is full of corrections and amendments. Many of the occupiers the second list were evicted only after an enforcement order was granted.

My main contribution has been to copy and re-index these lists, with a couple of changes. Firstly I have l out the sums of compensation, where they exist, partly for reasons of space. These were crucial at the tin but of limited interest now, and are very incomplete and confusing.

Secondly I have put the occupants at the head of the list. Originally the condemned properties we listed by address, then by owner, then by value, and last of all by the names of the families who actua lived there.

My order begins with the name of the titular head of the family, followed by the number in their househo at the time, their address, the owner of the property, the date they were evicted (if they were) and the da the property was actually demolished (if it was).

Where the record is incomplete I have indicated with an asterisk *. Where a planned eviction or demoliti did not take place, I have indicated with a dash —. The houses with a dash in the demolition column we therefore still standing when the records were handed over to Penwith District Council in 1974. It is e: to see how well the houses of owner/occupiers did in contrast to the rest. Identification of the individu dwellings is made no easier because so many of the older houses were not numbered. Everyone knew w lived where in 1937.

Despite the fact that these records are messy and occasionally confusing, I hope students will find much interest them here, from the local flavour of most of the names, to the numbers in the families, etc. I a hope that many local readers will find a small part of their own family history. Each entry represents human story, a house condemned as a 'slum', a family thrown into confusion, hope or despair. These are r dry lists, but the heart of the story of the *Rosebud*.

Appendix 1
REGISTER OF HOUSES IN CLEARANCE AREAS 1937 BY OCCUPANT

OCCUPIER & no in household	ADDRESS	OWNER	EVICTED	DEMOLISHED
P Allee (2)	Fishermans Square	Harvey, Dinsul, Heamoor.	02/05/38	3/51
William John Andrew (3)	St Peters Hill	Humphries, St Erth	20/06/38	
C Atkins (3)	3 The Fradgan	Chirgwin, Duke St, Newlyn	01/05/39	6/55
Arthur Balls (5)	Jack Lane	Carter, New Rd, Newlyn	20/03/39	—
Arthur Chas Barnes (3)	Church St	WC Brighton	09/05/38	3/51
Elizabeth Barnes (1)	Bowjey Hill	Occupier		3/51
T Barnes (?)	Dolphin Court	est ER Cara/St Austell Brewery	14/11/38	4/43
Misses EH & M Batten (2)	St Peters Square	Miss EH Batten		3/59
? Barnicoat (6)	12 Green St	H Simpson	25/10/37	*
The Misses Beckerleg (3)	St Peters Hill	Occupier	16/05/38	3/44
W Beckerleg (3)	St Peters Hill	White, Gwavas Rd, Newlyn	16/05/38	3/53
John & Mrs MA Blewett (6)	St Peters Square	Occupier	—	—
James Bone (3)	The Strand	Mabbott, Lane Reddin, Newlyn	22/05/38	12/50
*	St Peters Hill	Peter Bossalini (10 houses)	*	12/45
E Brown (6)	1 Factory Row	*	25/10/37	3/39
Louis Fred Brown (7)	St Peters Hill	John Frances	16/05/38	4/43
J Brownfield (3)	Green Rocks	Hichens, Green St	07/02/38	3/51
SG Brownfield (5)	22 Green St	White, Sea View Ho	25/10/37	*
Harold Button (7)	St Peters Square	Richards, Duke St	09/05/38	4/43
Elizabeth Clarke (5)	Fishermans Square	Harvey, Heamoor	02/05/38	3/51
Herbert Cobb (5)	Lower Green St	Samuel Deeble Tonkin	—	—
Joseph J Cock (7)	St Peters Hill	Curnow, Bay View Terrace, Newlyn	18/05/38	3/51
WP Cocks & EJ Harvey (4)	10 Bowjey Hill	Manning, Chyenhal	25/10/37	*
Mrs Bessie Cotton (3)	Lower Green St	Occupier	—	—
John Cotton (3)	Church St	WC Brighton	06/06/39	—
W J Cox (3)	5 Farmers Meadow	Hutchens Trust	27/03/39	3/48
WJ & Lizzie Dunn (4)	St Peters Place	Occupier	30/05/38	—
Mrs E Eddy (2)	12 Farmers Meadow	Hutchens Trust	20/02/39	9/48
James Eddy (4)	St Peters Hill	James Maddern	09/05/38	—
RS Eddy (4)	12/14 Bowjey Hill	Manning, Chyenhal	25/10/37	*
Edward Edwards (4)	Lower Green St	Mrs SH Strick	25/04/38	3/51
RG Ellis (3)	4 Navy Inn Court	H Simpson	25/10/37	*
Albert J Faull (2)	4 The Fradgan	Chirgwin, Bon Cot	30/09/39	6/55
John W Francis (7)	St Peters Hill	Occupier	—	—
Nicholas Francis (4)	Cairn William, St Peters Hill	RR Bath, Lidden	1/12/39	—
Elizabeth Gendall (5)	Fore St	Occupier	*	*
FC Gilbert (4)	1 Farmers Meadow	Hutchens Trust	20/03/39	3/48
J Gilbert (5)	7 Navy Inn Court	H Simpson	25/10/37	*
Mrs Mabel Green (3)	3 Duke St	Mabbot, Lane Reddin	20/02/39	12/50
WJ Green (2)	7 Farmers Meadow	Hutchens Trust	01/05/39	9/48
RC Grenfell (3)	Lower Green St	Thomas Williams	16/05/38	3/56
AH Hall (4)	6 Farmers Meadow	Hutchens Trust	27/03/39	9/48

Name	Address	Owner	Date	Date
TR Hampton (2)	4 Factory Square	White, Alma House	29/11/37	3/39
Caroline May Harry (4)	Fishermans Square	Harvey, Heamoor	02/05/38	3/51
Thomas Harry (4)	St Peters Square	Mrs Leah, Bude	16/05/38	3/51
William Harry (2)	St Peters Square	Mrs Leah, Bude	16/05/38	3/51
Mr ? Harvey (3)	Lower Green St	Tonkin, Lanoweth Rd, Penzance	25/04/38	3/51
Mrs Elizabeth Harvey (2)	Lower Green St	Mrs Elizabeth Wroath	08/08/38	—
JG Harvey (4)	10a Bowjey Hill	Manning, Chyenhal	25/10/37	*
Lizzie Mary Harvey (1)	Church St	James H Sexton	—	—
Mrs S Harvey (3)	2 Farmers Meadow	Hutchens Trust	20/03/39	3/48
TC Harvey (2)	2 Factory Square	White, Alma House	15/11/37	3/39
William Ernest Harvey(2)	Green St	Thomas Williams	04/04/38	12/54
Mrs WJ Harvey (7)	6 Navy Inn Court	H Simpson	25/10/37	*
J Hellewell (8)	Union Rd, off Jack Lane	Est ER Cara/ St Austell Brewery	23/01/39 (Taken into Dolphin Inn)	
E Hellier (4)	Lower Green St	Occupier	—	—
Alfred Hichens (3)	Church St	WC Brighton	16/05/38	3/51
John Hichens (2)	8 Green St	Occupier	31/03/39	—
Hannah Hitchens (1)	Primrose Court	Harvey, Street-an-Nowan, Newlyn	*	3/44
Phillip Hitchens (3)	St Peters Hill	Humphries, St Erth	09/05/38	—
Sidney Hitchens (8)	Vaccination Court	White, Alma House	09/05/38	9/47
Frederick Hocking (4)	Lower Green St	E Tonkin, Lanoweth Rd	25/04/38	3/51
Mr Horne (3)	Chywoone Hill	Hutchens Trust	*	3/48
Mrs Hosking (3)	5 The Fradgan	Thomas, Highfields, Newlyn	22/05/39	6/55
EJ Hosking (4)	6 Factory Square	White, Alma House	15/11/37	3/39
J Hosking (3)	2 Factory Row	*	07/06/37	3/39
Mrs V Humphries (5)	1 Factory Square	Cattrans	29/11/37	*
SW Ireland (5)	St Peters Square	Mrs Leah, Bude	16/05/38	3/51
JT James (1)	St Peters Place	Occupier	30/05/38	—
Ann Jenkin (4)	Dolphin Court	Est ER Cara/St Austell Brewery	21/11/38	4/43
William Jenkin (3)	Church St	W Jones, Church St	—	—
R Johns (2)	3 Factory Row	*	25/10/37	3/39
WJ Johns (3)	8 Bowjey Hill	Cattrans	06/06/38	3/39
J Jones (1)	2 Navy Inn Court	H Simpson	23/5/38	*
Mrs T Kelynack (1)	Farmers Meadow	Hutchens Trust	*	6/51
Peter Kitchen (7)	Cairn William, St Peters Hill	Mrs Hodge	09/05/38	—
Harold Kliskey (4)	Lower Green St	Tonkin, Lanoweth Rd	25/04/38	3/51
William Langstaff (4)	St Peters Hill	Tonkin, Carn Gwavas	16/05/38	4/43
F Larter (5)	7 Factory Row	*	25/10/37	3/39
L Lashbrook (4)	1 The Fradgan	Oliver, Mousehole	26/06/30	6/55
Edward Lawrence (3)	8 Farmers Meadow	Hutchens Trust	01/05/39	9/48
Annie Jane & William Rogers Leah (2)	Rhondda House, St Peters Hill	Occupier	—	—
Albert Maddern (7)	Vaccination Court	White, Alma House	09/05/38	9/47
B Maddern (4)	Meadow House, Farmers Meadow	Hutchens Trust	20/02/39	—
JF Maddern (3)	10 Factory Square	White, Alma House	15/11/37	3/39
Phillip Maddern (1)	Dolphin Court	John Cattran	—	—
Samuel Maddern (6)	Fishermans Square	Harvey, Heamoor	16/05/38	3/51
Samuel W Maddern (4)	St Peters Hill	Humphries, St Erth	16/05/38	3/51
T Maddern (4)	Farmers Meadow	Hutchens Trust	20/03/39	9/48
Blanche Matthews (1)	Fore St	Harold Hall, Greenbank, Penzance	16/05/38	—
George & Phyllis Matthews (5)	St Peters Hill	Occupier	—	—

JH Matthews (2)	Green St	Thomas Williams	25/04/38	*
John Henry Matthews(3)	Green St	Thomas Williams	16/05/38	3/56
JJ Matthews (2)	9 Bowjey Hill	Cattrans	04/07/38	3/39
Kate Matthews (1)	Church St	WC Brighton	20/08/38	3/49
Mrs Mary Jane Matthews (3)	Lower Green St	Occupier	—	—
Noel Matthews (3)	St Peters Hill	Humphries, St Erth	16/05/38	3/51
Thomas Henry Matthews (6)	Church St	WC Brighton	09/05/38	3/49
Elizabeth McDonald (2)	Dolphin Court	John Cattran	—	—
Annie McLary (2)	Church St	WC Brighton	09/05/38	12/43
Percy McLary(3)	Tonkins Court	W H Tonkin Sr	18/04/38	3/51
S Stanley Mildren (7)	St Peters Square	Mrs Leah, Bude	16/05/38	3/51
AJ Nicholls (8)	3 Navy Inn Court	H Simpson	15/11/37	*
Ernest Nicholls (4)	St Peters Hill	Mary Hichens	9/05/38	3/51
John R Nicholls (4)	Fore St	Richard Nicholls	*	*
Obed Nicholls (3)	St Peters Place	Occupier	30/05/38	—
Richard Nicholls (2)	Bowjey Hill	Occupier	—	*
Peter Olds (3)	Fore St	Hall, Greenbank	—	—
Edward C Osborne (2)	St Peters Hill	Humphries, St Erth	16/05/38	—
Grace J Paul (3)	St Peters Hill	Occupier	—	—
GJ Payne (6)	3 Factory Square	Cattrans	15/11/37	*
JC Payne (5)	Fore St	Drew, Mousehole	25/04/38	*
Mary Harvey Payne (2)	Lower Green St	Occupier	—	—
WGR Payne (9)	9 Factory Square	White, Alma House	17/01/38	3/39
Thomas Pearce (1)	5 Factory Square	Cattrans	15/11/37	3/39
Arnold Pender (3)	Fishermans Square	Harvey, Heamoor	16/05/38	3/51
Harold Pender (2)	Church St	WC Brighton	16/05/38	12/43
Maud Pollard (2)	Chywoone Hill	Hutchens Trust	*	3/48
J Pope (6)	12 Factory Square	White, Alma House	15/11/37	3/39
CHB Richards (3)	Lower Green St	Occupier	—	—
James & Mrs Richards (7)	Fore St	Occupier	—	—
Miss M Richards (2)	Jack Lane	John Cattran	—	—
W Richards (1)	St Peters Hill	Curnow, Bay View Tce	04/04/38	3/51
W Richards (4)	Farmers Meadow	Hutchens Trust	20/02/39	6/51
Wilfred Richards (3)	St Peters Hill	T Barnes, Fore St	06/05/38	4/43
W J Richards (2)	Lower Green St	Occupier	—	—
William M Robinson (3)	St Peters Hill	T Barnes, Fore St	22/08/39	4/43
William R Ross (2)	St Peters Place	Occupier	—	3/51
H Rouffignac (5)	Lower Green St	Tonkin, Lanoweth Rd	25/04/38	3/51
John Rouffignac (2)	Lower Green St	Hichens, Green St	*	3/48
J Rowe (3)	Lower Green St	Mrs S H Strick	*	3/52
John Rowe (2)	Lower Green St	Occupier	—	3/51
Alice Sampson (2)	Lower Green St	C H B Richards	—	—
Arthur Sampson (3)	2 The Fradgan	Oliver, Mousehole	26/06/39	6/55
Mrs EJ Sampson (2)	7 The Fradgan	Hitchens, Green St	(excluded by minister)	
T Sampson (5)	20 Green St	White, Sea View Ho	25/10/37	*
J Semmens (5)	10 Farmers Meadow	Hutchens Trust	27/03/39	—
James H Sexton (2)	Church St	Occupier	—	—
James H Sexton Jr (3)	Church St	James H Sexton Sr	—	—
Vivian Spargo (7)	Fore St	Messrs Pool & Son	*	—

Miss P Stevens (1)	14 Green St	Phillip White	14/02/38	*
Mrs Mary Stevenson (2)	Vaccination Court	White, Alma House	16/05/38	*
W Stone (2)	6 The Fradgan	Thomas, Highfields	30/11/38	6/55
William Stone (3)	Church St	WC Brighton	09/05/38	3/51
Clara Strowger (9)	Fore St	Harold Hall	31/01/38	3/44
John G Sykes (5)	Cairn William, St Peters Hill	Mrs Hodge, The Cliff	—	—
William Symons (4)	Lower Green St	Occupier	—	—
William Mark Symons (4)	Duke St	Mabbot, Lane Reddin	27/03/39	12/50
Miss Thomas (1)	Green St	Thomas Williams	20/06/38	12/54
John R Thomas (2)	Farmers Meadow	Hutchens Trust	*	6/51
Sidney Thomas (6)	St Peters Square	Richards, Boase St	09/05/38	4/43
Mrs Maud Thompson (1)	St Peters Square	Mrs Leah, Bude	25/04/38	3/52
Norman Tonkin (3)	18 Green St	Phillip White	25/10/37	*
Samuel Deeble Tonkin (2)	Lower Green St	Occupier	—	—
WH Tonkin Jr (4)	Fore St	W H Tonkin Sr	18/04/38	3/51
William Tonkin (6)	St Peters Hill	Tonkin, Sea View	30/05/38	4/43
JCB Trahair (5)	4 Factory Row	*	25/10/37	3/39
Walter Trahair (2)	Green St	Strick, Green St	30/5/38	9/47
WH Trahair (4)	8 Factory Square	White, Alma House	15/11/37	3/39
Mrs F Tregear (2)	Dolphin Court	est ER Cara/ St Austell Brewery	20/03/39	12/44
Albert Tregonning (5)	Church St	WC Brighton	16/05/38	3/51
Mrs Tregurtha (1)	Fore St	WH Williams, Fore St	20/06/38	—
Miss E Trevorrow (1)	Farmers Meadow	Hutchens Trust	*	6/51
WC Trewhella (5)	7 Factory Square	Cattrans	15/11/37	3/39
Joseph H Triggs (4)	Rose Villa, St Peters Hill	E & F Barnes	—	—
JT Uren (7)	1 Duke St	Mabbott, Lane Reddin	20/02/39	12/50
Mrs Bessie Wakfer (5)	Lower Green St	Occupier	—	—
E Wallis (1)	Dolphin Court	est ER Cara/ St Austell Brewery	31/03/39	4/43
Mrs N Wallis (2)	18 Green St	Phillip White	14/02/38	*
William Wallis (3)	4 Farmers Meadow	Hutchens Trust	20/03/39	3/48
Mrs Jane Waters (1)	St Peters Place	Occupier	*	3/52
Mrs PH Wearne (4)	Church St	WC Brighton	16/05/38	3/51
Robert Wearne (4)	St Peters Place	Grace James	09/05/38	3/51
WA Wearne (7)	5 Factory Row	*	25/10/37	3/39
Mrs A Welsh (5)	1 Navy Inn Court	H Simpson	25/10/37	*
James White (6)	9 Farmers Meadow	Hutchens Trust	01/05/39	9/48
Mrs H Williams (4)	Dolphin Court	est ER Cara/St Austell Brewery	21/1/38	4/43
Stanley Williams (4)	Vaccination Court	White, Alma House	25/04/38	*
Thomas Williams (3)	Lower Green St	Occupier	—	—
WJ Williams (2)	Green St	Thomas Williams	25/04/38	12/54
Thomas James Willis(2)	Lower Green St	Mrs S H Strick	25/04/38	3/51
Mrs Elizabeth Wroath (1)	Lower Green St	Occupier	—	—

Appendix 2
Housing Act 1936

REGISTER OF INDIVIDUAL HOUSES NOT REPAIRABLE (NOT IN CLEARANCE AREAS)

OCCUPIER and number in household	ADDRESS	OWNER	EVICTED	DEMOLISHED
WS Angove (4)	4 Trewarveneth St	WH Bone, Poole	24/10/38	—
William Angwin (2)	Church St	Lizzie Mary Harvey	26/06/39	—
Mr James Baker (4)	Back of Orchard Place	JH Nicholls, Morrab Rd	20/06/38	12/38
W H Baker (2)	Jack Lane	Mrs AP Rogers, Stockport	—	—
Mrs Bennetts (1)	Wesley Place	Arnold White, Sea View Ho	(Order 23/08/38)	10/10/38
			Taken into fish store	
GT Bennetts (6)	2 Foundry Lane	The Cara Estate	14/02/38	12/44
Mrs Berryman (3)	14 Fradgan Place	Arnold Snell, Trevilley, Bay View Terrace	19/09/38 Converted to garage and workshop	
Mrs S Berryman (2)	Orchard Place	B Rowe, Lyndale	—	—
Mr Blackburn (3)	Gwithiel Gwavas	J Wright	06/05/40	—
Mr Boase (4)	5 Roskilly Cottages	Penlee Quarries	14/11/38	—
Richard Bounden (6)	Boase St	Mrs S Hodge, PO, Fore St	(Order 03/08/38)	19/06/39
			(quashed 12/10/38)	
Mrs L Carbis (3)	Church St	WJ Johns, Church St	—	—
Wilfred Carbis (2)	Foundry Lane	est ER Cara	(Order 22/09/38) 31/07/39	12/44
C Carter (4)	Church St	WJ Johns, Church St	12/09/38	—
R Carter (3)	2 Vine Cottages	Mrs S Hodge, PO, Fore St	—	—
Mrs Chiffers (6)	Foundry Lane	P & E Beer, Chyenhal	(Order 23/08/38) 03/10/38	12/45
Mr M Cleverley (3)	St Peters Hill	A Rouffignac	20/06/38	—
Mr H Cobb (5)	Lower Green St	Samuel Deeble Tonkin, Lower Green St	31/10/38 —	06/78!
			(Closing Order 22/09/38)	
Mrs Cock (2)	The Coombe	Mrs Tregurtha, Vine Cottage	05/10/38	—
RT Cocking (3)	High Mountains	A & E Harvey, Boase St	15/08/38	—
Mr Coleman (2)	The Coombe	Mrs Tregurtha, Vine Cottage	31/03/39	—
Mrs C Cotton (5)	Gwavas Place	W Tonkin, Gwavas Ho	21/11/38	Converted
John Cotton (5)	20 Boase St	Thomas Cotton, Larrigan	15/08/38	—
Mr G H Curnow (2)	The Fradgan	T Barnes, Fore St	04/07/38	—
Mr Dan (2)	The Ope, Jack Lane	B Rowe, Lyndale	(used by Jelbert for ice-cream making)	
Mrs L Eddy (4)	The Fradgan	Arnold Snell, Trevilley, Bay View Terrace	12/09/38	—
WC Eddy (6)	Dolphin Court	St Austell Brewery	14/02/38	12/44
JW Edwards (2)	Church St	est Stephen Hitchens	(Order 10/08/38) 09/05/39	6/47
Angus Ellery (4)	1 Vine Cottages	Mrs S Hodge, PO, Fore St	—	—
Mr ? Ellis (4)	8 Eden Terrace	White, Sea View	12/12/38	—
Isaac Francis (1)	North Corner	H Weeks, N Corner	Deferred	—
John Francis (3)	Vine Cottage, Trewarveneth St	Mrs E Leah, Bude	30/01/40	*
William Francis (4)	Boase St	WM Trahair, Boase St	03/10/38	—
Alfred Frost (7)	High Mountains	JH Tonkin Ltd, Bread St	27/06/38	
J H Fry (4)	North Corner	Mrs C Kliskey, USA	(Order 13/10/38) 19/12/38	12/45
Sydney Gilbert (2)	Boase St	Mrs S Hodge, PO, Fore St	(Order 03/08/38 – quashed 12/10/38)	
Mr G Green (4)	The Fradgan	JH Nicholls, Morrab Rd	13/06/38	9/38

Name	Address	Occupier / Purchaser	Date	Date
John Green (4)	Gwavas Rd	Mrs Blewett, Fore St	22/05/39	3/51
Mr W Green (2)	The Fradgan	JH Nicholls, Morrab Rd	13/06/38	9/38
W Harbord (2)	North Corner	Mrs C Kliskey, USA	(Order 13/10/38) 01/10/38	12/45
Mesdames Harvey (5)	St Peters Hill	Occupier	20/06/38	—
Mr Abednego Harvey (3)	The Fradgan	Edward Tonkin, Fradgan	—	—
Alfred & Sarah Betsy Harvey (5)	Boase St	Occupiers	—	—
Arthur Harvey (4)	The Fradgan	Wright, Wherrytown	27/06/38	—
C Harvey (5)	Norfolk House, Fore St	Harvey, Heamoor	14/11/38	12/59
Mrs C Harvey (5)	3 Chapel St	Mrs E Richards, Hayle	—	—
Miss J Harvey (2)	Rear 8/10 Duke St	est M Kistler	—	—
James T Harvey &	Prospect House	James T Harvey	(Order 22/10/38) 24/10/38	12/44
Mrs Nicholas (two families) (7)				
Miss K Harvey (3)	Fore St	Harvey, Dinsul, Heamoor	—	—
Phillip (Rouffignac) Harvey (2)	Inglenook, Boase St	Mrs EH Rodda, PZ	(Order 16/08/38) 03/10/38	12/59
Mrs R Harvey (4)	Church St	est RT & RM Harvey	—	—
RC Harvey (3)	Boase St	JH Tonkin Ltd, Bread St	08/08/38	—
Thomas Harvey (3)	19 Boase St	Occupier	—	—
William Harvey (5)	Boase St	J Wright, Newlyn	14/03/38	—
F Henwood (3)	Gwavas Place	W Tonkin, Gwavas Ho	21/11/38 Converted	
A Hitchens (4)	Boase St	Stevens & Kelynack, Mo	(Order 03/08/38) 10/10/38	3/39
Elizabeth Hichens (1)	7 Eden Terrace	White, Alma Place	29/09/39	9/39
J Hichens (?)	Farmers Meadow	J Hichens, North Corner	renovated	
John Hichens (3)	Orchard Place	Cattran, Jack Lane	—	—
Miss Hosking (1)	10 Duke St	est M Kistler	—	—
James Hosking (2)	Foundry Lane	P & E Beer, Chyenhal	(Order 23/08/38) 24/07/39	12/45
Mr John Hosking (4)	The Fradgan	T Barnes, Fore St	11/07/38	—
William J Hosking (7)	Orchard Place	B Rowe, Lyndale	25/07/38	—
J Humphreys (3)	? 2 Church St	P & A Hichens, Victoria, British Columbia (Order 22/9/38) 17/10/38		
		converted to builders yard & office 1/44)		
Mrs Alice W Jacka (1)	Trewarveneth St	Treleaven, Coopers Court	21/03/38	*
FR James (4)	Coopers Court	Wm Bone, Poole	30/05/38	By owner
Robert James (1)	North Corner	M Paul, N Corner	11/07/38	—
Frederick Jasper (3)	The Fradgan	E Tonkin, The Fradgan	04/07/38	—
George Jeffery (4)	North Corner	M Paul, N Corner	30/05/38	—
C Jenkins (7)	North Corner	Mr C Kliskey USA	(Order 13/10/38) 19/12/38	12/45
Catherine Jenkins (2)	10 Boase St	Edwin & Elizabeth Rowe, Boase St	—	—
Mr J Johns (5)	St Peters Hill	Hosking, Fore St	30/05/38	
Richard Kelynack (3)	Jack Lane	Harry Ray, Dolphin Inn	12/09/38	
Thomas Kelynack (2)	Boase St	W Wright	11/04/38	—
WP King (4)	North Corner	Miss AP Pengilley	(Order 30/08/38) 10/12/38	12/44
John C Kneebone (2)	Farmers Meadow	Arnold Snell, Trevilley, Bay View Tce	*	03/48
E Lynn (5)	High Mountains	JH Tonkin Ltd, Bread St	15/08/38	12/38
Fred Maddern (2)	3 Boase St	JM Hitchens, Cliffside	22/08/38 (Taken into 'Cliffside' 3/56)	
Mr Maddern (?)	The Strand	Mr Badcock, The Strand	—	—
Mrs Maddern (3)	4 Roskilly Cottages	Penlee Quarries	—	—
Mrs H M Maddern (2)	9 Wesley Place	JH Nicholls, Morrab Rd	20/06/38	9/38
William Maddern (5)	Keigwin Court	TJ Harvey, Charles St	(Order 03/08/38) 12/09/38	6/49
William Mann (8)	? 4 Church St	P & A Hichens, Victoria, British Columbia (Order 22/09/38) 17/10/38		
		converted to builders yard & office 1/44)		

Name	Address	Occupier	Date	
WH Mann (2)	Gwavas Rd	Occupier	16/05/38 (Destroyed by fire 10/05/38)	
Fred Matthews (4)	The Fradgan	Edward Tonkin, Fradgan	—	
Harold Matthews (3)	North Corner	Mrs E Leah, Bude	(Order 22/10/38) 19/12/38	12/39
R Matthews (4)	11 Boase St	WJ Johns, Church St	—	
Mr Rodney Matthews (4)	10 Wesley Place	JH Nicholls, Morrab Rd	04/07/38	9/38
Walter Matthews (3)	North Corner	J Hichens, Green St	13/06/38	—
H A McGuiness (?)	Coopers Court	Occupier	—	12/55
Alfred McClary (2)	North Corner	W Tonkin, Helston	20/06/38	
George E McLary (3)	North Corner	Mrs A Pengilly, Tuckingmill, Cam	(Order 30/08/38) 15/08/38	12/44
Stanley Mildren (6)	North Corner	BJ Rowe Lyndale Chywoone Hill	(Order 30/08/38) 10/10/38 converted	
Alfred Minards (3)	North Corner	Mrs E Leah, Bude	(Order 22/10/38) 19/12/38 12/39	
Mrs K Mitchell (1)	3 Orchard Place	C Strick, Lane Reddin	28/11/38	—
W Nash (3)	Keigwin Court	TJ Harvey, Charles St	(Order 03/08/38)12/09/38	
			converted to workshop 6/49, since demolished	
Mr Netley (3)	Trewarveneth St	Mrs White, Ebeneezer Pl	12/09/38	3/48
RJ Nichola (7)	8 Fradgan Place	G Batten, Porthcurno	overcrowded included in clearances	
Mrs C Nicholls (1)	16 Trewarveneth St	JS Davies, Trewarveneth St	Deferred	(rebuilt)
Charles Nicholls (7)	Church St	WJ Johns, Church St	12/09/38	—
Mr Nowell (1)	Fore St	J Harvey, Heamoor	27/03/39	31/03/39
Mrs Oats (1)	The Fradgan	T Barnes, Fore St	21/07/38	—
Richard Payne (4)	North Corner	Mrs E Leah, Bude	(Order 22/10/38) 12/12/38	12/39
Miss Martha Pearce (2)	2 Boase St	JM Hitchens, Cliffside	22/08/38 (Taken into 'Cliffside' 3/56)	
W S Peck (7)	Wesley Place	Arnold White, Sea View Ho	(Order 23 08/38) 03/10/38	
			converted into studio)	
John Pentreath (4)	Keigwin Court	TJ Harvey, Charles St	(Order 03/08/38)17/10/38	
			converted to workshop 6/49, since demolished	
Mr Pilkerton (?)	The Strand	Mr Badcock, The Strand	—	
Bert Pitchers (2)	Jack Lane	Harry Ray, Dolphin Inn	12/09/38	—
TP Pollard (1)	Church St	WJ Johns, Church St	—	—
Mrs Potter (1)	North Corner	Cmd Bone, Poole	11/07/38	—
Alice Reynolds (3)	Trewarveneth St	Mr E Leah, Bude	(Order 22/10/38) 12/12/38	12/44
Frederick Reynolds (2)	Church St	Martha Downing, New Rd	*	—
James S Reynolds (3)	5 Trewarveneth St	WH Bone, Poole	25/07/38	—
Miss M Reynolds (1)	North Corner	Mrs C Kliskey, USA	(Order 13/10/38) 01/10/38	12/45
Nicholas Reynolds (2)	The Fradgan	J Reynolds, Fradgan	—	—
Nicholas Richards (3)	Boase St	Mrs EH Rodda, PZ	(Order 16/08/38) 03/10/38	3/48
William Henry Richards (5)	6 Trewarveneth St	WH Bone,Poole	25/07/38	
Miss Roberts (1)	Back of Orchard Place	Strick, Lane Reddin	—	—
Christopher T Roberts(2)	Coopers Court	Wm Bone, Poole	30/05/38	By owner
Jos Roberts (3)	6 Eden Terrace	White, Alma House	30/05/38	
Phillip Rouffignac (4)	6 Boase St	Occupier	— (Order 10/08/38) reconstructed	
			by Perrott, 5/56	
William Rouffignac (4)	5 Eden Terrace	White, Alma House	20/06/38	
Mr Rowe (4)	15 Fradgan Place	Arnold Snell, Trevilley, Bay View Tce	25/06/38	(by fire) 56
Mrs MA Rowe (2)	Boase St	Occupier	(Order 16/08/38) Deferred 39 —	
Mr Ruhrmund (4)	13 Fradgan Place	Arnold Snell, Trevilley, Bay View Tce	12/09/38 converted to garage and workshop	
C J Shears(7)	38 Boase St	Miss JM Mann, Gwavas Rd	05/09/38	—
E Simmons(3)	Church St	est Rt & RM Harvey	—	—
C Simons (4)	North Corner	BJ Rowe, Lyndale, Chywoone Hill	(Order 30/08/38) 10/10/38	—

Richard Simons (2)	North Corner	Mrs E Leah, Bude	(Order 22/10/38) 10/04/39		12/44
T Simons (3)	Church St	WJ Johns, Church St	12/09/38		—
TB Simons (4)	High Mountains	WJ Johns, Church St	12/09/38		By owner
WP Simons (4)	Church St	WJ Johns, Church St	12/09/38		—
Mrs M Smith (1)	The Fradgan	Arnold Snell, Trevilley, Bay View Terrace	12/09/38		9/56
Richard V Spargo(4)	Keigwin Court	Stevens & Kelynack, Mo	(Order 03/08/38) 10/10/38		3/39
HG Squires (5)	High Mountains	A & S Harvey, Boase St	15/08/38		—
Mr John Stone (3)	The Fradgan	Mr S Wright, PZ	20/06/38		—
W Stone (6)	8 Primrose Terrace	A White, Sea View	23/01/39		—
R Strick (4)	Jack Lane	Mrs AP Rogers, Stockport	17/10/38		6/58
Eric Strowger (4)	North Corner	Mrs E Leah, Bude	(Order 22/10/38) 05/12/38		12/39
Alfred Symons (4)	Jack Lane	Harry Ray, Dolphin Inn	12/09/38		—
Ernest Symons (4)	Dolphin Court	Harry Ray, Dolphin Inn	12/09/38		—
?Thomas (?)	7 Primrose Terrace	A White, Sea View	—		—
Mrs J Thomas (3)	The Fradgan	Arnold Snell, Trevilley, Bay View Terrace	12/09/38		—
JR Thomas (2)	The Meadow	Hutchens Trust	20/06/38		12/52
Norman Thorpe (3)	High Mountains	JH Tonkin Ltd, Bread St	15/08/3		3/39
Ed Tonkin Jr (6)	8 Chapel St	Edward Tonkin, Fradgan	30/05/38		—
J Trahair (2)	Orchard Place	W Tonkin, Helston	—		—
Mark Tredinnick (2)	Rear of Ice Works	Mrs Thomas, New Rd	—		—
WH Tregurtha (2)	Jack Lane	Mrs AP Rogers, Stockport	11/09/39	6/58	
SC Tremethick (4)	Boase St	Occupier	22/09/38	—	
William Treneer (3)	8 Duke St	est M Kistler	—	—	
Mrs Treneere (3)	12 The Fradgan	W Treneere, Fradgan	18/07/38	—	
William Treneere (3)	12a The Fradgan	Occupier	—	—	
Mark Tredinnick (4)	7 Boase St	R Pollard, Mousehole	(Order 10/08/38) 26/09/38 reconstructed by Perrott, 5/56		
Mrs Wakfer (1)	Rear 12a The Fradgan	W Treneere, Fradgan	—		—
J Wallis (8)	Orchard Place	J Nichols, Bread St	15/08/38		—
Thomas Waring (5)	Church St	est Steven Hitchings	(Order 10/08/38) 28/06/39		12/47
WC Warren (4)	Trewarveneth St	Mrs E Leah, Bude	(Order 22/10/38) 05/12/38		12/44
Robert Wearne (3)	Gwavas Rd	Mrs Blewett, Fore St	12/09/38	3/51	
Joseph Whitley (1)	Fore St	J Harvey, Heamoor	*	By owner	
Miss K Williams (4)	Orchard Place	B Rowe, Lyndale			
R H Williams (4)	6 Duke St	J Mabbott, Lane Reddin	24/10/38	3/59	
Richard Williams (2)	High Mountains	WJ Johns, Church St	12/09/38 By owner		
Stanley Williams (3)	Keigwin Court	Stevens & Kelynack, Mousehole	(Order 03/08/38) 10/10/38		3/39
Frank Wilmore (4)	3 Trewarveneth St	Mrs Williams, Tulse Hill	31/01/38	12/66	
Owen Worth (4)	Boase St	Basil Stevenson, Trewarveneth St	03/10/38	3/48	
J Wylie (3)	5 Orchard Place	JN Nicholls, Morrab Rd	12/09/38	—	

BIBLIOGRAPHY

Batten, Ben, *Newlyn Heritage*, Ben Batten 1980
Berriman, Hazel, *Cryséde – The textile designs of Alex Walker*, Royal Institution of Cornwall 1993
Corin, John, *Fishermen's Conflict – The Story of Newlyn*, Tops' Books 1988
Cross, Tom, *The Shining Sands – Artists in Newlyn and St Ives*, Lutterworth Press 1994
Fox, Caroline, *Painting In Newlyn*, Newlyn Orion Gallery 1985
Green, Iris M, *Artists At Home*, Iris Green 1995
Perry, Margaret E, *Newlyn – A Brief History*, Margaret E Perry, 1999
Pool, PAS, *A History of the Town and Borough of Penzance*, Penzance Corporation 1974
Stevenson, William, *Growing Up With Boats*, William Stevenson 2001
Watkiss, Reg, *Early Photographs of Penzance and Newlyn*, Peter Dalwood 1975
Williams, Douglas *Newlyn, Mousehole and Paul*, Bossiney Books 1988

Catalogue: *Thomas Cooper Gotch*, Royal Institution of Cornwall 2001